# CHARLES AND DIANA

# CHARLES
# AND DIANA

## Harry Arnold

NEW ENGLISH LIBRARY/TIMES MIRROR

For my wife Linda, and my children, Daniel,
Rachel and Rebecca – for everything.
And for Arthur Edwards, who made this book
possible.

A New English Library Original Publication, 1981

First NEL Paperback Edition April 1981

NEL Books are published by
New English Library Limited
Barnard's Inn, Holborn,
London, EC1N 2JR.

Printed and bound in Great Britain by
©ollins, Glasgow

All but two of the photographs in this book were taken by Arthur Edwards,
the Sun's royal photographer.

0 450 05332 6

# Contents

# Chapter One

## 'Who Will Be My Princess?'

'IF ONLY I could live with a girl before marrying her,' said Prince Charles. 'But I can't. It's all right for chaps like you. You can afford to make a mistake, but I've got to get it right first time. And if I get it wrong, you will be the first to criticize me in three years' time.'

Prince Charles was speaking to me at a small reception on the neatly manicured lawns of the British High Commission in Delhi in the autumn of 1980, as he began the most gruelling tour of his life.

He was also wrestling with the greatest problem of his adult life; and it involved a girl.

Those few words, spoken frankly by the Prince, revealed more than any other the very human dilemma he was facing. Quite simply, the question was: to marry or not to marry. Should he, as a man, simply choose a girl whom he could love for the rest of his days? Or should he, as the heir to the throne of the United Kingdom, choose someone he did not necessarily love but who possessed the extraordinary qualities required of a Queen? Most important of all, had he at last found the girl who fulfilled both requirements?

The tour of India was very much a 'make-up-your-mind' time for the Prince of Wales. A bachelor of thirty-two, he was under tremendous pressure – from his mother the Queen, from the British public and from himself. He was now saddled with his own deadline, having made the mistake of saying, just a few years earlier, that the age of thirty would be 'about the right time to marry'. That was in March 1975, when the Prince, at twenty-six, was playing the field and enjoying himself.

He had told a Parliamentary Press Gallery lunch at the House of Commons: 'I shall probably choose a girl much younger than myself.' He joked that he almost married . . . so as not to disappoint crowds who had read that his wedding was on the way. He was referring to his romance with Lady Jane Wellesley, daughter of the Duke of Wellington, whom he had only recently let slip through his fingers.

Said the Prince: 'I have read so many reports telling everybody whom I am about to marry that when last year a certain young lady was staying at Sandringham, a crowd of ten thousand appeared when we went to church. I almost felt I had better espouse myself at once so as not to disappoint too many people! As you can see, I thought better of it.'

The remarks were met by gales of laughter, but as time passed the joke was on Charles. For here he was five years later with no wedding banns in sight.

The Queen, for her own part, was anxious for her eldest son to wed as soon as possible and to produce an heir, *several* heirs. She had been thrust upon the throne by the very same sort of royal hiccup to which she now feared Prince Charles might fall victim. Her father George VI had become king only because his brother, the late Duke of Windsor, formerly King Edward VIII, had failed in his duty. He had committed the unforgivable sin of not only falling in love with a commoner (and a divorcée at that) but had renounced the Crown in her favour.

The smooth path of royal succession had been broken.

The Queen shares with her mother the belief that the death through cancer of King George VI was hastened by the burden and stress of his untimely elevation to the role of monarch. Nothing in his life had prepared him for it and his agony could be heard in the words he stammered to his mother, Queen Mary, when he was told of his brother's final decision to abdicate: 'B-b-but, I cannot even speak properly, Mama.'

It must never happen again. Of that the Queen was determined. The royal line must progress in safety, dignity and, above all, without interruption.

As part of that master plan, Prince Andrew has for many years been groomed as king-in-waiting, the chief understudy who would be ready to take over at a moment's notice if and when events demanded. Under the same plan the Queen ordered, early in her reign, that no two Royals, next to each other in succession to the throne, would ever travel by the same aircraft. Thus Prince Charles never flies with Prince Andrew, nor the Queen with Prince Charles. For an accident to interfere with such carefully thought-out determination was unthinkable. At all costs the blood of the House of Windsor must continue coursing through the veins of the monarchy into the twenty-first century.

In these later years of terrorism and violence, brought sharply and cruelly into focus by the assassination of dear 'Uncle Dickie', Earl Mountbatten, a sudden death could never be ruled out, nor could it be prevented. The Queen could only follow her self-imposed guidelines, and prepare a smooth path for her son's anointment by the Archbishop of Canterbury as King Charles III.

With subtle hints and the sort of gentle pressure with which all mothers will readily identify, the Queen had been steering the heir to the throne towards settling down and finding himself a bride. Now she was faced with an heir who couldn't or wouldn't choose a girl to help him produce an heir of his own.

The Duke of Edinburgh put his own oar into the muddied waters of Charles' romances. Never noted for his dulcet tones or diplomacy of words, Prince Philip told his son, gruffly: 'It's about time you got on with it. If you wait much longer, there won't be any suitable girls left – and you'll be on the shelf, my boy.'

Just how many of those thoughts were passing through Prince Charles' mind as he spoke to me in that Delhi dusk, we shall never know.

Certainly he was at a major crossroads. His long list of romances was fast becoming a joke. And he occasionally got into trouble with his mother for his zany antics in front of Press cameras – largely, I should add in fairness, with the encouragement of the Press themselves. But the Crown Prince was in danger of becoming the Clown Prince. He was also at a stage reached by many bachelors over thirty; if not quite crusty, he was becoming set in his ways, and a trifle selfish too.

At a royal dinner party in the Savoy in the summer of 1980 in honour of the Queen Mother's eightieth birthday, the Queen, surrounded by just about every other senior member of the Royal Family, sat tapping her foot – a classic sign of the sovereign's displeasure. She was waiting for the only missing member: Prince Charles.

It was an important celebration, and the Queen was furious with Charles for being late. 'We will start without him,' she said primly. And so they did.

In fact, Prince Charles was not very far away, at Windsor, getting in a few more chukkas of polo. His eventual arrival was greeted with a freezing stare from the Queen.

Polo is, like skiing, one of the Prince's true passions. But it is an expensive sport, not shared by the population at large. His string of polo ponies costs around £15,000 a year to maintain, and this, combined with his penchant for flying around the world in search of more sport and adventure, was earning him the reputation of a playboy.

True, the Prince has always worked hard. His annual list of public engagements is far longer than the general public appreciates, and he enters into each one as though it were his first, such is the genuine zeal he displays.

But he was, and is, a multi-millionaire without a particular career. He needs some £100,000 a year to maintain his lifestyle, and when he becomes king he will inherit the sovereign's fortune, estimated to be as large as £70 million. He may also inherit another fortune of several million pounds on the death of the eighty-four-year-old Duchess of Windsor. The ailing Duchess, bedridden at her home outside Paris, is understood to have named her late husband's great-nephew as her chief beneficiary, in gratitude for the kindness he has shown her since the Duke's death.

As to a career, Charles himself has said he knows it could be approaching the end of the century before he is crowned king. The Queen, who has never spent a day ill in hospital in her life, receives the best care modern medicine can offer, and can confidently be expected to reach at least the allotted three score years and ten.

There is a popular belief among the British people that the Queen will one day abdicate in her son's favour, and a recent survey has shown that the majority of people would like her to do so, giving Charles the opportunity to assume the throne while still a relatively young man. History vividly recalls how the matriarchal Queen Victoria never trusted her son, the Prince of Wales and, up to the moment of her death at eighty-one, refused to allow him to read a single state paper. The commonly held view is the present Queen would wish to avoid following Victoria's example. That much is true, but unless Prince Charles' marriage brings about the complete change of mind, the Queen will never abdicate.

I once held the same mistaken view that the Queen would stand down, and volunteered the thought to a Scottish peer who has strong connections with the Royal Family.

He disagreed and an animated argument developed. I pressed my point of view until he said quietly: '*Princess Margaret* doesn't think the Queen will abdicate.'

He didn't have to add 'And *SHE* should know.' The argument ended abruptly when I changed the subject.

Unlike Edward VII before his coronation, Prince Charles *does* read state papers, the Queen personally selecting those she thinks he should see, and forwarding them to him in a blue dispatch box. He will be perfectly familiar with the job when the crown is finally placed upon his head. But there is still the problem of the years in between. And marriage is an integral part of it.

Prince Charles, born at Buckingham Palace at 9.14 p.m. on Sunday, 14 November 1948, has been raised all his life with the understanding that it is his *duty* to marry.

He is not, after all, just anybody.

He is: Charles Philip Arthur George, the Prince of Wales, Earl of Chester, Duke of Cornwall, Duke of Rothesay, Earl of Carrick and Baron Renfrew, Lord of the Isles and Great Steward of Scotland, Knight of the Most Noble Order of the

Garter, Knight of the Most Ancient and Most Noble Order of the Thistle, Great Master and Principal Knight Grand Cross of the Most Honourable Order of the Bath.

The titles, of course, tell you nothing of the man.

Of the tens of thousands of people who have personally met him, I have never come across one who actually disliked him. To men and women alike he has a dashing air; he can discuss almost any subject under the sun; he loves a good joke and can swap the 'blue' variety as well as any naval stoker. As well as polo and skiing, he loves the opera, painting in water colours, fox-hunting and pheasant shooting.

He never smokes and seldom drinks, though he does have a weakness for the occasional glass of pink champagne. He is keen on physical fitness and regularly exercises, with stretching routines, in the privacy of his Buckingham Palace quarters. He is a light eater, preferring a plain omelette to an exotic dish, and in recent years has become almost a vegetarian.

He is an admirer of: the American singing group The Three Degrees, Lauren Bacall, Barbra Streisand, and Shirley Bassey who, on his thirty-first birthday, gave him a photograph of herself with the handwritten message 'My time is your time.'

But there is a tetchy side to him too, and bachelorhood made him tetchier by the year. He is particularly sensitive about the dignity of the monarchy. Woebetide anyone who refers to the Queen as 'your mother' and, although he will good-humouredly tolerate being addressed as 'Your Majesty' by mistake, he will cut dead anyone who casually calls him 'Wales'.

He can also be very short with his personal staff. On one occasion he pelted socks at his valet when he was handed the wrong pair. 'I don't like the bloody colour!' he shouted.

He is a stickler for routine, inherited partly from the Queen but also from the strict regime at Gordonstoun School where he grew accustomed to a spartan existence, bordering on the sadistic, which included *two* cold showers a day. If you can set your watch by the Royal Family, as many courtiers claim, then you can set the second hand by Prince Charles.

When he retires at night, he leaves strict instructions about the time he should be awakened. On overseas tours, when he often sleeps on aircraft, the timing can be crucial if he is to rise and be prepared, in full military uniform an hour later, to meet a head of State or perhaps a king. Any member of his staff who neglects to rouse him at the exact appointed time is likely to receive a verbal lashing he will not easily forget.

The woman who marries Prince Charles will find he is not all sweetness and roses. Even in private he has insisted his girl-friends call him 'Sir'.

By the autumn of 1980, the Queen was encouraged by signs that Prince Charles was at last showing signs of settling down. For one thing, he had finally found a home of his own.

It was no small matter, for Prince Charles could not live in his cramped Buckingham Palace bachelor quarters for ever. Once married, he must have a London home, and in the fullness of time he will inherit Clarence House, across the Mall from the Palace. But he must also have a country retreat, a 'family home' where he can raise his children.

Originally, he was to have lived in Chevening, a Palladian mansion standing in 3000 acres near Sevenoaks in Kent. Why he never moved in is a mystery which may now be explained. The glorious house, with its thirty-six reception and state rooms, marble floors and Waterford cut-glass chandeliers was bought by the first Earl of Stanhope in the reign of George I. When the seventh Earl died without an heir in 1967, he left it to the nation, together with a trust fund of about £250,000 to provide for its upkeep. The Earl, who had met Prince Charles several years earlier, also left a memorandum to the Prime Minister expressing his wish that the house should be first offered to the Prince.

But centuries had taken their toll on the once beautiful home, and when Prince Charles and the Queen made a tour of inspection together in 1969, they found it in a gloomy state of disrepair, the façade crumbling and the once-fine Italian

13

plasterwork falling from the walls. They turned down the offer. Four years passed, and the Prince said 'No, thank you' again after one wing had been made habitable. Lord Hailsham spent one winter in the new wing until the fall of the Government forced him out of the Lord Chancellor's office. After £250,000 had been spent transforming the house Prince Charles finally and reluctantly agreed to live in it. It was not easy for the Prince of Wales to leave his parents' home, where he had been cocooned all his life.

The Prince made further visits with the Queen and set about planning the furnishing but, as the months drifted by, his enthusiasm waned. Local villagers were annoyed by the fact that he called so infrequently – and even when he did, he arrived and left by helicopter so that no one saw him. As far as is known he never set foot outside the estate. The Prince had come to realize that the mansion, though surrounded by lush countryside, was close to none of the pursuits of which he had become fond: the polo fields of Windsor and Sussex, the hunting country of Beaufort and the Belvoir and the testing course of Badminton – all were too far away.

This problem could have been resolved by making more frequent use of a helicopter, but there was another, overwhelming reason why Prince Charles never moved in. Chevening, in the words of senior Kent police officers I spoke to, was a 'security nightmare'. They had discovered that the estate had so many unprotected approaches that it would have been impossible for them to safeguard his life. They calculated that it would take a permanent team of twenty-four officers to maintain an adequate, round-the-clock guard. I have personally walked, with a Special Branch officer, along a footpath which crosses the estate to a point which has a perfect view of the front entrance, 200 yards away. The spot could have been tailor-made for a sniper.

Chevening was rejected as unsafe and, in the wake of Earl Mountbatten's assassination only four years later, security advisers to the Royal Family are confident they made the correct decision.

Prince Charles seemed as far away as ever from settling

down in a home of his own until, in the early part of 1980, he discovered Highgrove House, near Tetbury, in the rolling Cotswolds.

Highgrove has nothing of the sumptuousness of Chevening, but it was its very unpretentiousness which first attracted the Prince. Its nine bedrooms, six bathrooms and nursery wing may sound impressive to anyone living in a two-up, two-down, but to a man of Charles' riches they are the minimum.

The house cost the Prince £1 million, less than it would have eventually cost to restore Chevening totally, and it stands in a modest seven acres with a few stables and out-buildings. Most importantly for the Prince, it is less than two hours from London via the M4 and is conveniently placed for reaching Cornwall where the Prince's Duchy responsibilities often take him. Highgrove is in the middle of Beaufort Hunt country – and Badminton, with its horse trials, is only a short drive away.

Moreover, the Prince, when he moves in, will have 'instant neighbours'. Gatcombe Park, the home of Princess Anne and Captain Mark Phillips, is within easy reach, as is the home of Prince Michael of Kent.

Prince Charles has been through a difficult time with his brother-in-law, Captain Phillips, who rejoices in the nickname, earned in the Army, of 'Fog'. During the early years of Anne's marriage, Prince Charles would refuse to come down to breakfast at Buckingham Palace if Anne and her husband were staying overnight there, insisting instead on a tray being sent to his rooms. But in recent years, the rift has been healed with the birth of Master Peter Phillips, Princess Anne's son. Prince Charles was godfather at the christening and dotes on the boy, visiting him whenever he is in the area.

Highgrove, Prince Charles' Gloucestershire hideaway, may have played a significant part in bringing Charles to terms with his future and the need to find a bride, for the crucial autumn of 1980 found the Prince in a strangely changing mood. He had, in the words of one senior

Buckingham Palace courtier 'sobered-up' (not, of course, in the drinking sense). The catalyst in the change may have been the presence of the Hon. Edward Adeane who, eighteen months earlier, had succeeded Squadron Leader David Checketts as the Prince's private secretary.

The role of private secretary to a monarch-in-waiting has none of the usual routine connotations of answering letters, arranging appointments or dealing with minor details. It is a vital office which can only be filled by a man with sufficient courage to give firm advice to the highest prince in the land, and have the nerve, if necessary, to say, 'No, you cannot do that', when some hare-brained stunt is afoot.

David Checketts, who had served the Prince for nine years, helping him through his schooldays, his years at university and his naval career, is said to have left because he fell out with Charles towards the end. I have also been told that Mr Adeane was appointed specifically at the Queen's request to help 'tone-down' Charles' image as a ladies' man and a prankster. There is probably some truth in both accounts. At any rate, Mr Adeane, a friendly, efficient man with the mild-mannered air of a Sunday school teacher, and a razor tongue sheltering behind it, brought a new look to the Charles camp.

Edward Adeane gave up a successful career as a libel barrister – with such incompatible clients as the Tory Party and *Playboy* magazine – to serve the Crown. Although I never had the pleasure of hearing him in court, he must be gifted with a formidable power of persuasion. Whatever the reason, the Prince's image *did* change. His sense of humour was still there – no one would want, for a moment, to crush it – but in his working life he became more serious in his approach.

Royal engagements began to have a heavy look about them: civil engineering institutes, heavy machinery factories and City of London associations began to appear on the 'Wednesday list' – the official programme of the Royal Family's public duties issued by Buckingham Palace. All were worthy of a Royal visit, of course, but if the deliberate

16

aim was to bring some sobriety into the Prince's life, then it worked.

Commoners other than Mr Adeane have influenced the Prince of Wales in his adult years. Among them is his small team of bodyguards, supplied by Scotland Yard's Royal Protection Squad, and headed by Chief Inspector John MacLean. Throughout their lives, members of the Royal Family spend more time in the company of their respective policemen than with their own relatives. The experience is a rewarding one, for the plainclothes officers are the first true touch of reality experienced by the Royal Family, who for the most part live in a false world behind chintz-curtained windows of palaces and great houses.

An ordinary boy learns the realities of manhood through the mutual exchange of gossip and boasting – much of it invented – with his contemporaries. But who is there to tell a prince what life is really all about? He is in a race apart, remember, naturally reticent in contributing his own thoughts and views for fear they may be reported back, and used against him. Royal bodyguards, on the other hand, are not only experienced men of the world but, through the nature of 'the job', are sworn by means of the Official Secrets Act to total secrecy. Members of the Royal Family are safe, therefore, to confide in them. Not about State matters, of course, but about themselves.

Chief Inspector MacLean is one of the few men who has shared at least some of the Prince's private thoughts over the years and who, in subtle ways, has helped him mature. The two men have an extraordinarily close working relationship. One a Prince, the other a policeman – men poles apart – they have a similar sense of humour, share a love of the outdoors and enjoy a passion for skiing.

Each February, when Prince Charles heads for the ski slopes of Klosters in Switzerland, Chief Inspector MacLean accompanies him, his gun hidden in a leather pouch strapped around his waist. The two men have improved their skiing together to the point where both are considered first-rate. During these winter jaunts in the snow, the police officer becomes almost a member of the Royal Family, staying in the same tiny wooden chalet, and sitting at the same table with the Prince. A man with his feet 'under the table', as it were.

John MacLean, a wiry Scotsman with a solid frame you would not wish to meet in a dark alley at midnight, is like a particularly nasty tiger when angered, but for the most part he is a genial, happy-go-lucky extrovert with an earthy sense of humour which amuses the Prince. Having been at the Prince's side for some twelve years, he always – without exception – calls him 'Sir', but he is also able to speak freely to the Prince, without pausing to choose his words. The Prince calls him, in public, 'Officer', but in private the burly policeman is 'John'.

There is a particular story about the two men which illustrates better than any other the affinity between them. Possibly apocryphal, it has a ring of truth about it. One evening, Prince Charles and Officer MacLean were driving through Glasgow in a Range-Rover, the Prince at the wheel. The Chief Inspector suddenly pointed down a dark side street, and said casually to the Prince: 'My mother lives down there.'

'Does she really?' said Charles. 'Let's pop in to see her,' and made to turn the wheel, an impulse typical of the man.

MacLean looked at his watch and, in mock seriousness, said 'No, I'm afraid we've missed her. She'll be out mugging cripples by now.' The two men roared with laughter as they drove on.

The Prince's thoughts have also been shared in recent years by the Palmer-Tompkinsons – Charles, always called Charlie to avoid confusion, and his wife Patty – a charming and friendly couple, who rent the Swiss chalet where the Prince takes his annual skiing holiday (Charlie, an ex-Olympic skier, has tutored the Prince in the finer points of the sport). They rank among his closest friends, and during the skiing holidays live with him like a family.

Prince Charles enjoys the company of married couples, and particularly married women, because he knows he is safe from rumours of romance. He can talk confidentially to a married woman and be seen in her company – as long as her husband is also around – without getting into the gossip columns.

Patty, a vivaciously attractive woman in her late thirties, is one of the Prince's few real confidantes. Round a log fire in the Swiss chalet, the Prince has been able to look at his future and consider the prospect of marriage in the company of a happily married couple who have a family of their own. To Charles, their advice is of a value money cannot buy.

Lord and Lady Tryon are another 'substitute family' Charles has shared over the years. Tony and Dale are his hosts every August in their fishing lodge on the River Hofsa, near Egilsstadir in Iceland, and, every day for two weeks, Lord Tryon, a director of a London merchant bank, will stand at the Prince's side up to the waist in freezing water fishing for salmon, while the Prince's detective sits on the river bank reading a novel. Around them the countryside is desolate, the trees stunted by the low temperatures and the ground rock hard. Civilization is a two-hour drive away on an unpaved road. The holiday is not everyone's idea of fun, but the experience is one which is likely to bring two men close together. The talk, not surprisingly, is more about fish than anything else.

But there is time, in the evenings, safe inside the fishing lodge, for talk of other things – of life, love and marriage. Tony's Australian-born wife Dale, blonde, bubbly, attractive and extrovert, is one of the women closest to Charles. He affectionately calls her 'Kanga', his jokey word for 'kangaroo', and there are few princely secrets she does not share.

Tony has been a friend of the Prince since childhood and Charles is godfather to their three-year-old son who is his namesake. Dale, who is also the mother of twins, is one of the few women who can actually get away with poking fun at the Prince when he joins them for dinner at their home on a 700-acre estate near Salisbury, Wiltshire. She says of the fishing expeditions: 'We always have a terrific time. The Prince

19

enjoys being able to get away and relax completely.'

Dale, and one other married friend, Camilla Parker-Bowles, have acted as an unofficial 'vetting committee' to the dozens of girls who have flitted in and out of Prince Charles' life. If a girl did not past muster with Dale and Camilla, she did not stay at the Prince's side for long. As women, they were able to detect in a girl faults to which Charles was blind.

Camilla is married to dashing Andrew Parker-Bowles, a Royal Household Cavalry officer, who was once an escort of Princess Anne. A polo-playing friend of the Prince, his six-year-old son Thomas is also one of Charles' godchildren. The Parker-Bowles are another couple whose home in Gloucestershire is close to Highgrove.

In the tight circle of the Prince's trusted friends, the golden rule is 'discretion'. To break the code of silence and talk about the Prince to 'outsiders' is to lose his friendship for ever. But the Prince selects his friends carefully and, once chosen, they are likely to remain friends for life. He once said: 'I trust my friends implicitly. And they know it. The more discreet, the more trustworthy they are, the better. Those people who do get drawn into conversation and do natter about me find they get into the papers. But I hear they don't get paid much.' The iciness of the comment reflects the value Prince Charles places on total loyalty.

He, naturally, confides in his parents. He has, in particular, a powerful bond with the Queen – deeper than that of any ordinary mother and son – because of their unique destiny. One a sovereign and the other a sovereign-in-waiting, they have a special understanding no one else can share. In time, Charles will also know the isolation of the monarch, at once close to family and friends, but distanced from them by the aloofness of the crown.

But there are some problems he cannot discuss with his mother, notably those concerning affairs of the heart. As a boy, he was close to his father and, although the two still have a deep love and respect for each other, Charles has tended to grow a little away from Prince Philip as the years have passed. In moments when he is unable to resolve a nagging problem, or when it is *himself* he wishes to discuss, he turns to the one member of the family with whom he has a very special relationship: the Queen Mother.

Queen Elizabeth the Queen Mother has long been a favourite of the nation. She, more than any other, guided the Royal Family through the rocky seas of the Abdication crisis in the late 1930s. Later she was stalwart support for the people of Britain through the dark years of the war, walking beside her husband through the blitzed East End of London and commenting, after Buckingham Palace was bombed, 'Good. Now I feel I can look the East End in the face.'

The Queen Mother has never been quite able to disguise the fact that Charles is her favourite grandchild, and Charles, for his part, simply adores her. Her thoughts and advice have carried a great deal of weight as the Prince prepared himself to choose a bride.

But if the Queen Mother is his closest *confidante*, then his closest *confidant* was dear 'Uncle Dickie', Lord Louis Mountbatten, until his tragic assassination by IRA terrorists on 27 August 1979 at Mullaghmore, County Sligo, Ireland. He had been holidaying with his family on their boat, *Shadow V*, when a bomb – hidden on the boat – exploded, killing him instantly. This senseless and obscene act also took the lives of his fourteen-year-old grandson Nicholas, and a boatman of seventeen, Paul Maxwell.

The Earl was closer to Charles than some men are to their sons. He was the only man I ever saw put his arm affectionately round the Prince in public. He also gave the Prince advice about the choice of a wife and would listen sympathetically to Prince Charles' own thoughts on the subject. The Earl's dearest wish was that his own flesh and blood should be linked with the monarchy, and he urged the Prince to consider marrying one of his granddaughters, Amanda and Joanna Knatchbull. Charles dutifully did so – but, sadly for the Earl, nothing came of it.

After Mountbatten's death, Prince Charles reacted in a way which would surprise many who do not truly know him. His face twisted in anguish and rage, he shouted: 'I'd like to

21

put on a uniform, go over there and kill some of those bastards!' They were rash words, spoken in anger and in private, but they were also the words of a man, and a soldier. Later, when the initial shock had passed, he reflected on the problems of Ulster and said quietly: 'We really must try to do something . . . something.' It would be totally in character if, behind the scenes, Prince Charles were to put forward some suggestion for a new initiative in that strife-torn province which has been a running sore in the nation's side for almost 300 years.

Prince Charles never knew either of his grandfathers. His paternal grandfather died before he was born, and when King George VI died, the Prince was little more than three years old. So he 'adopted' Lord Mountbatten as his grandfather, and when the Earl was buried, Prince Charles sent a wreath with a message in his own hand: 'To My H.G.F. from your H.G.S.' The initials stood for 'Honorary Grandfather' and 'Honorary Grandson.'

As the Prince of Wales went about his official engagements in the weeks following the funeral, he seemed, to those of us covering his programme, a changed man. His great-uncle's death undoubtedly had a deep and lasting effect on Prince Charles. If any single event was calculated to make him consider again his role in life, his future and the whole question of a family of his own, it was the Mountbatten tragedy.

As the months went by, Prince Charles gradually pulled himself out of the mood of profound sorrow in which the tragedy had left him, and his old humour returned. But as his thirty-second birthday approached, the India tour behind him and another year ahead, the thoughts and advice of his friends and family – all those who loved him – converged into focus. It was his *duty* to marry. And a sense of duty is a quality Prince Charles possesses in a measure second only to that of the Queen.

He was, in any case, tiring of the chase, to put it bluntly. For many years it had been fun to play the field, to find a new girl-friend as quickly as the old one was discarded. No man had a greater choice, when the hunt began. But now the field was getting smaller every day.

'Whenever I give a dinner party these days,' he confided gloomily to a friend, 'More and more of the guests seem to be married.'

He had also hugely enjoyed a cat-and-mouse game with Fleet Street, smuggling girls into and out of his life. If a girl was spotted and photographed, that was a point against him. But if she eluded the Press altogether, that was a point in his favour. As a game of pure fun, it had had its high moments.

But the joke had worn transparently thin.

There was however one other reason why Prince Charles' mind had been concentrated of late on the subject of taking a bride. He had met a girl. Or rather he had rediscovered a girl he had known for many years. The enlightenment had occurred just a few months earlier in the summer of 1980. And now he realized that he was falling in love with her. The incredible thing was that, after searching all his adult life for the girl he could make his Queen, it had happened out of the blue.

Alone one weekend, Prince Charles had been idly dwelling on a pheasant shoot he had particularly enjoyed three years earlier . . . He had been introduced to her in the middle of a ploughed field. 'She was only sixteen then, but she was such fun.'

The Prince of Wales paused for a moment, then reached for the telephone.

# Chapter Two

### DIANA: 'Born to be Queen'

IF LADY Diana Spencer was heaven-made for Prince Charles, then her father, the eighth Earl of Spencer, certainly gave the angels a helping hand.

For that matter, any one of his three daughters could be regarded as 'ideal' for marrying into the Royal Family. From birth, each of the girls was groomed to make what is still old-fashionedly termed a 'good marriage'. Historians will no doubt reflect that Lady Diana was a perfectly obvious choice from the start. Hindsight is, of course, a wonderful thing and Prince Charles, for one, would have been saved a great deal of heartache had he been blessed with it.

A close look at her background is invaluable in contemplating her future.

The Earl's ancestry is full of Royal connections, with a noble family tree which links him to more than one king. Few families can boast such a proud lineage. Charles and Diana themselves are sixteenth cousins, once removed, through their shared ancestor Henry VII. The Spencer family – motto: 'God Defend the Right' – dates back to the sixteenth century when Warwickshire-born John Spencer – who, like his descendants after him, made a fortune from sheep farming – was knighted by Henry VIII.

Robert, the first Lord Spencer, was made a baron in 1603, and became one of the richest men in the land. His grandson, Henry, was created the first Earl of Sunderland by Charles I as a handsome 'thank you' for the £10,000 he lent the King at the outbreak of the Civil War. The Earl was killed only four months later at the Battle of Newbury, and the second Earl became adviser to three kings in succession, Charles II, James II and William III. While the senior branch of the family went on to become the Dukes of Marlborough, the junior branch became the Spencers. There are also links with the Churchill family, the Earl of Lucan who helped write-off the Light Brigade in the Crimean War, and the celebrated Prime Minister Robert Walpole.

The Spencer girls, as they say, have plenty of history but no past. The present Earl Spencer continued the royal tradition of loyalty and service, and when his daughters came along they found they were the Queen's Norfolk neighbours.

The Earl had been equerry to George VI from 1950 until the King's death and later to his daughter, the Queen. She let him end his service to her and return early from a royal tour to prepare his wedding plans in 1954. It was natural, therefore, that, when the ceremony took place in Westminster Abbey in the June of the same year, the Queen – who had been crowned only two years earlier – was, with her husband Prince Philip, among the 1700 guests.

The Earl's bride was Frances Ruth Burke Rocha, daughter of the fourth Baron Fermoy. Incredibly, their marriage created a precedent for the romance which was to blossom twenty-six years later – for the bride was twelve years the junior of the bridegroom and in those days such a gap was, if not quite a scandal, not exactly the 'done thing' either. The way was more than paved for the acceptance of the age-gap of nearly thirteen years which exists between Charles and Diana.

The couple quickly settled down to producing a fine family. The Spencer's first-born was Lady Sarah, who arrived in 1955. Long afterwards, it was to seem for a while that Sarah might be 'the one' for Prince Charles, but their brief romance ended when headstrong Sarah became one of the few girls to actually turn down the most eligible bachelor in the world before he had even had a chance to ask her! It was in May 1980, three years after that romance ended, that Lady Sarah married ex-Coldstream Guards officer, Old Harrovian Neil McCorquodale, the son of printing millionaire Alastair McCorquodale. The girl who just might have become Queen helps him run a farm in Grantham,

Lincolnshire, on his parents' estate.

The middle daughter, Lady Jane, was born in 1957, and like her sister grew up to make a 'good marriage'. Her choice was Robin Fellowes, the son of the Queen's agent at Sandringham, who has also known the Royal Family and their children all his life; he was formerly Prince Charles' private secretary, and is now the Queen's assistant private secretary. Thus another link was forged in the intricate chain which binds the Spencers to the Crown.

The selection of godparents over the years has made the links even stronger. The late Queen Mary and the late Duke of Windsor were godparents to the present Earl, and the Queen is godmother of Lady Diana's brother Charles.

Lady Diana was born at Sandringham on 1 July 1961, and was christened there by a former Bishop of Norwich. She was not exactly the most welcome bundle of joy to arrive in the world on the hottest afternoon in fifteen years for, after the tragic death of a baby son, her parents had hoped for another boy. So determined were they to produce a male heir that they had not even thought of a single girl's name. Their son, Charles, was eventually to complete their bliss on 20 May 1964.

Earl Spencer, like any father, planned a bright future for his children, but royal weddings seemed a long way off in those childhood days when the 'Queen's House' was just the other side of a low wall. Looking back, it is difficult to see how Prince Charles could have overlooked Diana, for she was literally 'the girl next door'. The age-gap probably had a great deal to do with it for, though they first met as children, it was as a 'splendid sixteen-year-old' that Diana was to be first recalled by the Prince.

This meeting was in November 1977, when Prince Charles went, as a friend of Sarah's, to the family home for a shoot. Sarah introduced them in the middle of a ploughed field and later, quite justifiably, declared herself Cupid in the royal love match.

Lady Diana then regarded herself more as part of the Prince Andrew set, for they are the same age. 'I always

26

ganged up with Andrew,' she cheerfully admitted later, though the two never dated, as has been suggested in some quarters. In fact, Diana knew all the Queen's children. Sandringham, the Queen's Norfolk estate, lacked one attribute dearly loved by all children – a heated swimming pool. The Spencer home, Park House on the Sandringham estate, did have one, however, and it was the royal children who would ask to 'come over for a dip'.

The Queen actively encouraged the royal children's friendship with 'the Spencer girls' and to Lady Diana the Queen was always 'Aunt Lillibet'. The Queen Mother, in particular, thought the Spencer children to be 'fit and interesting' company for her own grandchildren. Indeed, she had such a high opinion of the Spencer family altogether that at one time or another she appointed all four of Lady Diana's grandparents as her personal courtiers. Diana's maternal grandmother is still a lady-in-waiting at Clarence House.

So it was that Lady Diana, the shy one of the four youngsters, grew up totally unawed by the presence of royalty. She was asked just before the engagement: 'If you walked into a room and found yourself confronted by the Queen, the Duke of Edinburgh, Prince Charles and the Queen Mother, would you feel nervous?'

Diana replied: 'No, of course not. Why should I?' Her surprise at the question was totally genuine, for the whole of her upbringing and training had prepared her to meet royalty on an equal footing, certainly as far as protocol and manners were concerned. Members of the Royal Family no more overawe Lady Diana than Mr and Mrs Jones next door intimidate you or me. In many senses the Spencer children *are* royal.

Diana was perhaps lucky in being the third-born of her family. Few parents of two or more children are unaware of the fact that the first-born inevitably suffers the anxieties of learner-mothers – and fathers. While mum and dad learn the ropes – even with the help of doting nannies – the first baby invariably acts as a guinea-pig. The second child follows a long-established path. And the third enters such a relaxed, 'seen-it-all-before' atmosphere that he or she tends to have a happy-go-lucky childhood. According to many experts on the subject, it is for these reasons that first-born children often grow up to become pioneering world leaders, for the simple reason that they blaze the trail for those who follow them. The comparison with trail-blazer Lady Sarah is irresistible.

Second-born children, according to the same proposition, tend to be more relaxed individuals, while the third takes on a positively poetic nature. Strangely, psychologists believe that the pattern repeats itself with the birth of the fourth child. Fourth-born Charles, Viscount Althorp, who will one day become the ninth Earl Spencer, may help us in time to judge whether or not the theory is correct.

As to the third-child phenomenon, it can only be recorded that Lady Diana is a lover – like Prince Charles – of art, poetry and music, and is remembered by her first governess, Gertrude Allen, as a 'very happy and relaxed child'. Miss Allen, now in her seventies, would sit with baby Diana for hours on end in the nursery rooms of Park House, listening to her first words, patiently helping her with her mistakes and tolerantly clearing up behind her, though generally she recalls her as 'a tidy soul'.

Had the gentle Miss Allen known that she was entrusted with the responsibility of raising a future Queen to the English throne, she in turn might have been overwhelmed by the prospect. On second thoughts though, the dutiful Miss Allen – a treasured example of a fast-dying breed – is honest enough to tell how it really was. 'Well,' she carefully explains, 'I wouldn't say that Diana was particularly bright as a child, but' – and now with conviction – 'she was a real TRYER.'

In 1969, when Diana was just eight years old, the calm and order of her life was rocked by an event which, until comparatively recent times, could have automatically disqualified her from ever becoming the wife of a king: her parents were divorced.

There is no 'good age' for a child to suffer the trauma of its parents breaking their wedding vows but, if anything, Diana was slightly luckier than her sisters who were old enough (Sarah was fourteen and Jane was twelve) to understand and be hurt by what was happening. Nevertheless, the divorce had a deep and lasting effect on the youngest girl. Her friends believe it explains, in part, her love for children.

'It's as though she wants to protect them from the pain she suffered through her parents' divorce, and make them feel more secure than she did,' one friend explained.

The biggest complication – and perhaps embarrassment – for Diana, arising out of the divorce, was to come many years later when even the skills of the Lord Chamberlain, Lord MacLean, the man responsible for planning great state occasions, were taxed to the full in deciding who should sit where in St Paul's Cathedral.

There was a note of weariness, born of experience, in Lady Sarah's voice when she commented on the seating problems: 'I suppose it will be the same as it was at my wedding and my sister Jane's, when my parents sat together. God knows how it will be sorted out. I pity the poor person who has to do it.'

Lady Diana's mother was named as the co-respondent in the divorce of wallpaper millionaire Peter Shand Kydd and his wife Janet. In the sixties, long before divorce law reform, the female partner cited in such an action was popularly known as the 'other woman' – a tag which carried a prejudicial implication of immoral behaviour. Children can be the cruellest beings on earth and it is likely that the older Spencer girls, at least, were teased about the divorce at school.

The divorce went through, and Diana's mother married Mr Shand Kydd. The Earl had earlier been awarded custody of all his four children. But as the Spencer children settled down to their new life, another shock, possibly a greater one, awaited them in the years ahead. In 1975, when Lady Diana's father – then Viscount Althorp – succeeded to the earldom, the family moved to Althorp Hall, in Northamptonshire. A year later, the bombshell dropped.

'Daddy' was going to take a new wife, in the formidable form of Raine, who was then the Countess of Dartmouth.

And there was no gentle breaking of the news.

Raine, a forceful woman even in her calmer moments, came into young Diana's life with all the subtlety of a hurricane. Her previous marriage, too, had been the victim of a teenage wedding. She was eighteen when she married Gerald Legge, then a twenty-four-year-old Guards Officer and Earl Spencer's Old Etonian schoolfriend. A powerful 'do-gooder' in her day, Raine put as much enthusiasm into her desertion as she had into her marriage until the glitter wore off: she moved lock, stock and barrel into Althorp Hall and reorganized the servants overnight. It was the Earl's turn to be cited in the Dartmouth's divorce which swiftly followed and, when they were married a few months later, Lady Diana – and her sisters – boycotted their father's wedding.

If the stepmother were not enough, the children also 'inherited' another overpowering relative: Barbara Cartland, the colourful, if not slightly eccentric, romantic novelist, who became their stepgrandmother. Miss Cartland could be competing with Dickens for the title of England's most prolific writer, such is the volume of the outpouring from her pen. What she lacks in quality, she more than makes up in quantity and, were there to be an Author's Olympics, Barbara Cartland would undoubtedly write for England.

If Miss Cartland had only had her way, Prince Charles would have met a beautiful princess years ago. They would have fallen in love the moment their eyes met, and he would have carried her off to his kingdom on a white charger. Miss Cartland's positive plethora of novels includes, ironically, *Bride to the King*, which contains the breathless lines: 'Tonight, my darling, you are only a child, and not yet a woman, and that is why I want you to think that I am the Prince of your heart, just as you are the Queen of mine.'

Lady Diana, one of the world's greatest blushers, would no doubt take on the deepest hue in the history of embarrassment were the words ever read aloud to her. But, as no man is his brother's keeper, so no man or woman can be held responsible for their grandparents – inherited or otherwise. And in the words of another old saying: A man marries a woman, not her family.

Royal history moves at such a pace that it is easy to forget the lessons of modern times. It is worth noting, therefore, the experience of Captain Mark Phillips after his marriage to Princess Anne. Although his parents were, of course, given pride of place in Westminster Abbey, and welcomed afterwards to Buckingham Palace, since then there has been little evidence of familiarity between the Phillips and the Royal Family.

Miss Cartland is unlikely ever to grace the balcony of Buckingham Palace. For one thing, her huge hats would get in the way. As a retired royal-estate worker I once met put it: 'There's Royals, and there's Royals. Then there's those who ain't.' It would be an optimist of Micawber proportions, therefore, who would expect Raine and Earl Spencer, Barbara Cartland and the Shand Kydds to be welcomed into the homes of the Royal Family, once the necessary nuptials are over.

For their own part, the Spencer girls – with Diana taking an increasingly headstrong line – set the pace in the turmoil which disturbed their teenage years, and which may yet provide the blueprint for the future.

The Queen, I know from personal experience, has a stare which can kill at twenty paces, though I am pleased to say it has never been directed at me. Diana and her sisters dealt with their unwelcome 'step-relatives' in a similar style which begs to be faulted: they ignored them.

One of the injured parties protested her pain: 'I want us all to be one close family,' said Raine, 'but they are all so against me. Whatever I do is wrong – they won't accept me.'

The former countess has still not been really accepted, and the girls have remained close to their real mother, even though she lives 500 miles away with her husband on a farm at Oban, Argyll. The strained relationship between girls and stepmother has been slightly improved in the last two years, however, following a massive brain haemorrhage suffered by their father. Only a woman of Raine's determination could have nursed, cajoled and almost bullied him back to health; the Earl still suffers from a slight slurring of his speech following the stroke, but otherwise declares himself 'fit as a fiddle' and his children know they have their stepmother to thank for it.

If the lack of security in Lady Diana's family background did little to prepare her for the demanding role she now faces, her schooling was a model of stability. She would probably have made a terrible shorthand-typist, but her education did give her more than just academic ability. Her world was broadened considerably as she discovered that not all playmates were children of the Queen, and she began to develop an extraordinary ability to mix easily with everyone she met.

After attending a primary school at King's Lynn, Norfolk, where little is remembered of the toddler, she moved on to Riddlesworth Hall, a preparatory school at Diss in the same county. Her headmistress was Miss Elizabeth Ridsdale and, although now retired, she remembers the leggy Diana among the thousands of children who passed through her hands. It was Diana's ability to fit in so easily and – even at that tender age – her loving care for smaller children, which Miss Ridsdale recalls.

'What stands out in my mind,' she said, 'is how cheerful and kind she was with the youngsters. Everyone seemed to like her. She was always a decent, kind and happy little girl and I'm pleased to say that is how she has gone into her adult life.'

When she was thirteen, Diana, then something of a gawky girl, was enrolled as a boarder at the £3000-a-year West Heath School, in Sevenoaks, a 130-pupil establishment thought then, by the upper middle classes, to be *the* school for girls of good breeding.

Diana's father – formerly Viscount Althorp – had by now succeeded to the title, and the family were living in Althorp Hall, in Northamptonshire. Her schooldays were interspersed with long holidays at Sandringham.

No one would claim Diana was a genius at school. Academically, she was 'average, or perhaps slightly above' and is remembered best as 'jolly keen at sport'. She tried her hand at tennis, hockey and lacrosse, and if she didn't excel at any she was regarded as a useful team member; she was also a particularly strong swimmer. But once again it was her pleasantness and cheerful disposition which struck both the staff and the girls around her.

A boarding school can be a lonely place for an impressionable teenager and West Heath – like any other school – had its share of girls sobbing in the dormitory at night as they suffered the pangs of first separation from their families. Diana not only coped with her own feelings and adapted readily to the life, but comforted others in their loneliness.

Diana took no 'A' levels and at sixteen wanted to leave school. Her father put his foot down and said she must stay but, after some gentle persuasion from Diana, agreed to her alternative suggestion that she should go instead to a finishing school in Switzerland. The move was a fortuitous one, for she was to learn the skills which would stand her in good stead for later years.

She became fluent in French, a language spoken by virtually all the members of the Royal Family with at least a moderate degree of skill. During official visits to France, the Prince of Wales speaks in French both socially and for the purpose of delivering speeches, and dozens of Frenchmen I have spoken to during such visits have been glowing in their praise for his French which, they have said, is spoken with almost no accent.

Diana also became an accomplished skier, which could well be regarded as an essential qualification for any girl wishing to capture Prince Charles. His own skiing ability is exceptional, and for several years he has perfected his style with a two-week visit each February to the ski resort of Klosters in Switzerland.

Lady Diana remembers her days in Switzerland as among

the happiest in her life. After her return to England she was never to be quite so free again. With a little time to spare, she took up riding but never really mastered the art. 'I fell off a horse and lost my nerve,' she confessed later. She fights shy of any suggestion that she should take it up again, though Prince Charles is likely to encourage her as much as he can, if only so that she can keep up with his equestrian activities.

But if riding is not a love she shares with the Prince, music is. Charles is an accomplished cello player and she a more than passable pianist. The arts, too, are a shared interest.

Diana, like her sisters, was never a debutante. The traditional 'coming out' custom was at that time rapidly disappearing – the Queen always hated it – and in any case Diana was not one to enjoy the falseness and boredom of 'doing the rounds' of the social season.

She returned briefly to Althorp Hall – a stately home, incidentally, which would leave none of its residents overawed by the size of Buckingham Palace. The home of the Spencers since 1506, its 15,000 acres speak for themselves, but the sheer magnitude of the house has to be seen to be believed. Inside is an astonishing collection of art treasures, including 700 paintings by artists such as Gainsborough, Van Dyck and Rubens. Althorp (pronounced, by a beautiful piece of English idiosyncrasy, as 'Altrup') is now the Mecca of £1.00-per-head tourists.

But even as a young girl, Diana was never over-impressed by it. Like any other child in any other house, Diana was fond of nipping down to the kitchen – in this case, several kitchens – when nobody was about, to see what she could sample from the larder. She also started to cook for herself in the Great House, and developed a culinary skill which came in useful during her days as a bachelor-girl in London. Now, as a princess-in-waiting, she doesn't even need to know how to cook an omelette unless she particularly wants to.

At seventeen, even the vastness of Althorp made the freedom-loving Diana feel cramped and she yearned to set up a home of her own. Money, of course, was no problem and Earl Spencer readily paid out around £50,000 for a generously proportioned three-bedroomed flat at Coleherne Court in Old Brompton Road, South Kensington. (The flat is now worth twice that sum.) Diana quickly found three flatmates: Virginia Pitman, Carolyn Pride and Anne Bolton. For the two years they were together, the St Trinian's atmosphere of a girls' dorm filled the flat, as each began to carve out a career.

A fierce loyalty and devotion also developed between the 'four musketeers', as they regarded themselves – and in time Anne, Virginia and Carolyn were to share a royal secret for which any Fleet Street man would have given his eye-teeth.

From the beginning, they laid down firm rules about sticking together. The number one rule was 'no poaching boy-friends'. Not that any of them were boy-mad. Instead, they shared their spare time with each other. When they were not popping down the Fulham Road to the ABC cinema, or spending an hour or two sharing a bottle of wine in a nearby pub, they were at home watching television.

The flat was gloriously untidy, with skis, tennis racquets, bikes, as well as clothing, lying in odd corners. The kitchen was invariably full of washing up and, although they took turns at tidying-up, Diana is remembered by the other three as the tidiest of them all – 'you know, not exactly fastidious, but organized.' On one occasion, the three remember, Diana was unwell and stayed home for the day. But she could not bear the thought of doing nothing for a whole day, so she went through the flat from top to bottom, making all the beds, washing-up, even taking care of the laundry.

Lady Diana also found her first job. She joined the 'Young England' kindergarten in a church hall in Pimlico, South London, where toddlers from relatively high-born families daub paint, scribble in scrapbooks and generally play to their hearts' content to the tune of £180 a term. The nursery is run by two of Lady Diana's old schoolfriends, Vicky Wilson and Kath Seth-Smith. 'Miss Diana' was an instant hit with the children – it was always to her they first wanted to show their work, and during one 'lesson' they all attempted a portrait of her.

It was the sort of job that will always earn Diana tributes in the future for the loving care she gave the youngsters, and when her 'great day' came I know Diana was sad to leave.

Unknown to any but her closest friends, Diana also spent nearly a year caring for a young handicapped boy. The boy, named Patrick, aged two, lived in Eaton Square with his American parents who lavished love and attention upon him. But he needed extra stimulus, and when Diana heard of him she readily volunteered her help. Unsung and unpaid, she visited him two afternoons a week to help take the strain off his parents. She would take him for outings in his pushchair, or just sit and talk to him for hours on end. Some time towards the end of 1980, the little boy returned with his parents to America, much the richer for the time kindhearted Diana had devoted to him. His departure left, for a time, an emotional gap in Diana's life and she filled it, typically, by offering herself as an unpaid nanny, nursemaid and babysitter to several other very young children.

On the happy day that, God-willing, Lady Diana gives birth to a child of her own and hopefully, a future monarch, the demands of babyhood will not be unknown to her. Natural mothers are not created. They are born and – blessedly for the British monarchy and Charles himself – Lady Diana is one of them.

In the years to come, Lady Diana is certain to recall those kindergarten days with deep nostalgia and perhaps the odd pang of regret for 'what might have been'. Without dispute, Lady Diana's marriage to Prince Charles will bring her the greatest fulfilment of her life but nothing will ever match the satisfaction she felt in caring for young children.

They were also the last of her carefree hours: driving around London at will in her distinctive red Mini Metro; popping into Fortnum and Mason for tea; sorting through the dresses at Harrods and planning each day as it arrived. In future, her days will be planned weeks in advance.

Above all else, Lady Diana approached the end of her teens, like her sisters before her, with an unsullied reputation. Her father had done all he could to send her into

36

the world without so much as a faint blur on her character, but once in London, it was very much up to Lady Diana herself. Whether or not she had hopes, a premonition even, of what was to come, she lived up to her father's expectations, and kept her character stain-free.

She never had a steady boy-friend. Indeed, we have still to read the name of any young man who claims even to have taken her out on a date. She eschewed the nightlife. Tramp, Wedgies and other 'nightspots' were not what Lady Diana was seeking. Not once did her name figure in a gossip column, a difficult enough achievement in itself for someone with such royal connections.

Diana, herself, has never pretended she had any particular ambition. Happy with her work, her life and her love of children, she might have continued to work at the kindergarten for many more years. She might have met a Guards officer or a stockbroker, and settled down for a life in the country and an untitled family of her own. She might have disappeared into obscurity. Except for a telephone call.

Lady Diana had returned from London to Althorp to spend a weekend with her father, as she occasionally did, when the call came through. 'Hello Diana,' said a voice. 'This is Prince Charles. Would you like to come down to Sussex to watch a game of polo?'

# Chapter Three

### Interlude

POLO DOES not attract the sort of crowds which flock to stadiums throughout Britain every winter weekend to watch soccer and rugby matches. A 'gate' of 500 would be an exceptionally good day at Smith's Lawn, Windsor, or at Midhurst, Sussex, home of the Cowdray Park Polo Club, where Lady Diana sat watching the Prince at play on that Saturday in July. Most of the spectators had club passes; if the survival of the sport depended on public support, it would have died years ago.

The 'car park' had a different look about it, too, with vehicles stationed around the field itself. Rolls Royces were outnumbered only by estate cars, most of them carrying hampers of cold food – chicken, grouse and the like – squashed in among useful quantities of white wine. There was a stand of sorts, but families – with more titles among them than you could shake a stick at – favoured standing or sat on car bonnets.

Lady Diana was enthusiastically egging on *Les Diables Bleu*, The Blue Devils, the Prince of Wales' team, who were clearly in danger of losing the match. She sat in the private members' enclosure, next to the clubhouse, with a small group of friends. It was a dull, classically English summer's day – no sun but no wind either – and Diana wore an opened-neck blouse and a thin flared skirt similar to one which was to cause her great embarrassment many months later. Around her neck on a chain was a gold initial 'D'.

Between chukkas, Prince Charles returned to the pony lines and swapped sweat-soaked shirts as well as mounts. It was, and is, among the few occasions that the general public can, if they wish, view the hairs-apparent on the royal torso.

But not once did the Prince acknowledge the girl he had

specially invited for the weekend. At the end of the match, he left the polo ground in his royal blue Ford Granada Estate, with a silver polo-pony mascot on the bonnet. Lady Diana left in a separate vehicle and joined him at the nearby home of his old friend Commander Robert de Pass. They spent the rest of the weekend together and parted early on the Monday morning.

Even in the small crowd of about two hundred which gathered at Midhurst that weekend, Lady Diana might have escaped unnoticed and their secret first date might never have been recorded. But I was there as Royal Correspondent of the *Sun* newspaper together with Arthur Edwards, the newspaper's top photographer. Neither of us realized the significance of Lady Diana's presence at the game, but Arthur – who spotted her among the spectators – took a photograph. It was never published – nor did I write any copy – but it was filed away in the *Sun*'s picture library, just in case it should become significant later . . .

# Chapter Four

## Press Relations

THE ROYAL FAMILY of Britain and Fleet Street's Pressmen have been inextricably bound together since the day that William Caxton cured the teething problems on his printing press.

The British people have, as a general rule, an insatiable appetite for stories and photographs of the Royal Family, and newspapers have for many years attempted to satisfy that appetite. It must also be said that the Royal Family appreciate, too, the importance of the Press to their own existence. Without the media, how long, would it be before the Royal Family slipped from public popularity, as has happened in other European countries in our own lifetime?

Conscious of their public image, the Royals, and the Queen in particular, plan their foreign tours with careful regard for the necessary media coverage. In a series of briefings before a tour takes place, reporters, photographers and television crews discuss the tour programme in a code-language unknown outside Fleet Street: UFP (unlimited fixed point), MLP (moving limited pool) and NF (no facilities), all help photographers understand where and where not they may take photographs. But their presence on a tour is essential. Why, for example, should the Queen go through the exhausting experience of shaking hundreds of hands in a far-off nation, if the British people know nothing of it?

In 1979, when the Queen undertook a tour of four African countries, the Government of Malawi made it clear that Pressmen would not be allowed to accompany the Queen over its borders. Buckingham Palace replied to the Malawian Government – in suitable diplomatic language, of course – that it was a case of: No Press, No Queen. The bar was withdrawn and the tour went ahead.

Difficulties arise over the coverage of the Royal Family's private lives and Fleet Street tries hard not to overstep the mark in the pursuit of matters which are genuinely in the public interest. Where to draw the line is a problem which has never been properly resolved. Who is to say whether the very public relationship between the Queen's sister, Princess Margaret, and erstwhile pop singer, landscape gardener and unemployed Welshman, Roddy Llewellyn, justifies reporting on the Princess's private life? Is it right that, if Fleet Street had not made its own discreet inquiries, the divorce of Princess Margaret and Lord Snowdon would not have been known to the British people until Buckingham Palace chose to make the announcement?

In many situations, both the Royals and the Press walk a tightrope, and in the last fifty years this dilemma has produced many classic Fleet Street stories and headlines.

During the first part of the century when Fleet Street was totally ruled by Press barons, American and Continental newspapers often pioneered the way by telling their readers important stories about the British Royal Family of which the British people themselves knew nothing. Thus it was that the American people knew months before the British of the love affair between the late King Edward VIII and American divorcée Wallis Simpson, and of his plans to abdicate because of her.

The crisis produced one of the most memorable headlines of all time when the *Chicago Sun* reported on the divorce between Wallis and her husband Ernest. The divorce had, with the help of the King, been quietly slipped into the Causes List at Ipswich, where Wallis had taken up the necessary residence, and where it was hoped the hearing would be missed by Fleet Street. The Chicago newspaper learned of the divorce hearing, discovered that Ipswich was the birthplace of Cardinal Wolsey, and employed in its headline a slang expression based on an American city famed for 'quickie' divorces. It blazed: 'King's Moll Reno'd in Wolsey's Home Town.'

Fleet Street proprietors had maintained a conspiracy of

silence over the affair which was never to be tolerated again.

Many years later, the Royal Family was facing its first major crisis since the Abdication as Princess Margaret wrestled with the problem of whether or not to marry Group Captain Peter Townsend, also a divorcé, with whom she had fallen in love. The *Daily Mirror*, under the famed editorship of Hugh Cudlipp, kicked over the traces, and covered its front page with the headline: 'Come on Margaret, make up your mind!'

Mr Cudlipp later justified this as a 'friendly shout from the crowd' and in many ways that is what it was. Its effect will never be known but, in the event, Princess Margaret turned down the Group Captain and went on to a disastrous marriage with a man of whom everyone approved.

In the coverage of their personal lives, members of the Royal Family have had to learn individually how best to cope with it. The Queen has seldom, if ever, put a foot wrong in public and a 'bad Press' about her is practically unknown. Prince Philip once turned a hosepipe on photographers – at an official engagement, too – and has made headlines from time to time with his generous use of four-letter words. 'Turn that f— siren off!' he screamed at an unfortunate police officer during the Queen's tour of Saudi Arabia, thumping the car roof to emphasize his request. Fleet Street had a field day, but Prince Philip is respected for his human qualities as well as his failings, and his outbursts are enjoyed rather than tolerated – four letter words and all.

Princess Anne has never learned how to handle the Press or the public. Her critics could be forgiven for believing that, like a petulant pop star, she enjoys the fame but not the publicity, the privilege but not the hard work required to deserve it. At public engagements she can be charm itself to her hosts, and they are left wondering why she has such an awful reputation. But she has a gift for rubbing up the wrong way the ordinary people she meets in her day-to-day life. Other members of the Royal Family groan when they read of her latest gaff.

She once shouted at a group of anti-hunt demonstrators,

as she rode to hounds: 'Who's paying you to do this?'

'No one,' came back the reply, 'but we are paying *you* to do *that*.'

When the Queen bought her daughter Gatcombe Park, in Gloucestershire, a Buckingham Palace servant who has to put up with her temper on a personal level, remarked that it was 'to get her as far away from London as possible'.

'Not far enough,' said another, bitterly.

The Queen Mother's superb Press relations need no elaboration here. She has a graciousness and calm which is born of her very make-up, not forced through necessity. She is one of the very few Royals for whom hard-bitten Fleet Street photographers will collect for a gift on her birthday, or when she is unwell. The Duchess of Kent, incidentally, is another. And in both cases, they have personally expressed their thanks.

Second only to the Queen Mother from whom he learned a great deal, Prince Charles probably has the best working relationship with the Press. That says a great deal, considering the overwhelming interest in his activities.

Intense Fleet Street coverage began from the moment of his birth, and when he was still a toddler the Queen had to ask Fleet Street picture editors to withdraw their photographers because it was interfering with his schooling. The picture editors obliged, as always, but the respites have always been brief. It is a tribute to the Prince's character and courage that as he grew up, and the going got tougher, he maintained an amicable – sometimes Christian-name – relationship with Pressmen. He blows hot and cold, of course, and occasionally blows his top, as he is entitled to. But he quickly cools down again and is very forgiving to those who have angered him.

His real problem began when he began his quest for a bride. He was living in an era of attitudes totally different from and freer than those of his forebears, and he began his courtship under the lenses of carefully-focused Nikons. From the moment Prince Charles first noticed the attraction of the opposite sex, Fleet Street editors recognized the spectacular exclusive (the word 'scoop' is never used in Fleet Street) which hovered over their front pages.

Which newspaper would be the first to name the future Queen of the United Kingdom; and which would capture the royal coup of modern times by correctly predicting the engagement announcement? In the cut-throat circulation war between the popular newspapers, few stories held such promise in terms of prestige. In the search for that golden prize several mighty clangers were dropped.

The most famous was when the *Daily Express* announced across its front page: 'Charles to marry Astrid. Official.' The Luxembourg princess had for some time been firm favourite in the Prince Charles marriage stakes, but the *Express* was not over-concerned with the fact that the Princess is a Catholic which disbarred her from marrying the Anglican Prince.

The story, which appeared on a Friday, declared authoritatively:

> Prince Charles is to marry Princess Marie-Astrid of Luxembourg. The formal engagement will be announced from Buckingham Palace on Monday. The couple's difference of religion will be overcome by a novel constitutional arrangement: any sons of the marriage will be brought up according to the Church of England, while daughters will be raised in the Catholic faith.

All hell was let loose, both in Fleet Street and at Buckingham Palace. Prince Charles was furious over the story. Through the Palace Press office, he issued a personal denial. It stated: 'I am authorized by His Royal Highness, the Prince of Wales, to make the following statement. There is no truth at all in the report that there is to be an announcement of an engagement of the Prince of Wales to Princess Marie-Astrid of Luxembourg.'

And when Fleet Street persisted, through enquiries to the Palace press office, that the denial did not rule out the possibility of an announcement on another Monday, John Dauth, the Prince's press officer, was moved to say, 'They are not getting engaged this Monday, next Monday, the Monday after, or any other Monday, Tuesday, Wednesday, Thursday or Friday. They do not know each other, and people who do not know each other do not get engaged. The Royal Family do not go in for arranged marriages. If the Prince and Princess have met at all, then it has been briefly at official functions.'

That was that. The *Express* had got it horribly wrong, and had made it twice as hard for anyone else ever to get it wrong again.

The story behind the *Daily Express* exclusive-that-never-was is a fascinating one in terms of the way Fleet Street sometimes obtains its information. The *Express* had been sure of its facts, because they came from an 'impeccable source'.

The phrase is over-worked in Fleet Street but for once the phrase is justified, for the man who supplied the tip-off was a member of one of the highest governing bodies in the land, an organization of top-ranking individuals who cannot be named in these pages. Scotland Yard's Special Branch, which is responsible for internal security, had suspected for some time that there was a 'mole' on the Committee who was supplying Fleet Street with information which, if not classified, was of a highly confidential nature. Special Branch officers singled out a short list of suspects and began to test each one in turn by deliberately leaking him or her sensational, but totally false, information. The officers then sat back to wait to see if the 'story' turned up in Fleet Street. If it did not, of course, the individual had vindicated himself.

They had reached only the third person on the list, and had fed him with the Marie-Astrid story when the *Daily Express* splashed it the following day. The outcome was an unhappy one. The man concerned quietly resigned his office, and the *Daily Express* lost a first-class source of information. Only Fleet Street reporters, and perhaps senior police officers, know how hard such an informant is to find, and it is part of the workings of our democracy that reporters are permitted to use information gathered in this manner, as long as the Official Secrets Act is not broken.

Prince Charles' denial over the Marie-Astrid story was the first and last he ever made, He felt he had to issue it because of the compelling way the story was presented, and particularly because of the word 'Official' at the end of the headline. But to have adopted the habit of issuing denials each time his name was linked with a potential bride would have been to run headlong into a trap. For the moment he failed to follow the pattern, and a denial was unforthcoming, then everyone would know *this* was the girl.

Prince Charles has never been a man to have anything to do with deceit; nor has he ever forgotten the row which followed the announcement of Princess Anne's engagement to Captain Mark Phillips. Up to the last moment, staff at the Buckingham Palace press office continued to issue statements, often bad-temperedly, that there was no romance. Afterwards the credibility of the press office was at its lowest ebb for many years. Prince Charles made up his mind that it would never happen in his case, and he vowed, too, that no one would know of his engagement before the official announcement. Eventually, he went so far as to ensure that he was never photographed with his bride-to-be. Charles was not going to make it easy for Fleet Street.

But the betrothal of the Prince of Wales remained, for Fleet Street, a world-exclusive looking for an owner.

After the Anne and Mark business, nothing could be taken on face-value. The engagement, too, of Princess Margaret to Lord Snowdon had caught everyone napping. Clearly a new approach would have to be adopted. The Prince would have to be more studiously reported. The time would not be wasted, for the Prince has, in any case, been 'good copy' since his moment of birth.

His sense of humour and adventurous lifestyle have secured him more column inches in recent years than the Queen herself. He has only to kiss a girl, however innocently; tell a joke, however badly; or make a gaff, however small — and he is instantly on the front page.

'Prince Charles,' chief sub-editors would say, 'walks into the paper.'

With that in mind, several far-sighted editors ordered discreet, but intensive, coverage of Prince Charles' activities away from the public eye. Without encroaching unfairly upon his privacy, news desks instructed reporters to keep a careful eye on the girls he met during his weekends away from public engagements, and to watch for the signs of a significant romance. Prince Charles was to lead us all a merry dance in the years which followed. Red herrings were to swim in shoals before the cameras.

With the full backing of its then immensely successful editor Sir Larry Lamb, the *Sun* entered wholeheartedly into the race to be first. Sir Larry, who had taken the *Sun*'s circulation from a deathbed 850,000 to around four million – the biggest daily readership in the English-speaking world – suggested the need for a permanent 'royal team', a reporter and photographer who could watch and study the day-to-day movements of the Prince, and maintain a continuity which could one day be a decisive factor. The suggestion, as events later proved, was a momentous one.

Press coverage of the Royal Family had never been developed as a specialist subject in Fleet Street, except inasmuch as the same photographers tended to represent their newspapers on overseas tours. But none of their work was of an investigating nature, nor did they concern themselves with anything other than *public* engagements. There were, therefore, no ground rules to follow, no hints on how the task should be approached.

Through the former news editor, Ken Donlan, now editor of the *News of the World*, and later his successor Tom Petrie, the style of the *Sun*'s royal coverage was honed to perfection with journalistic skill and professional integrity. The pioneering work, on the reporting side, was carried out for the *Sun* by James Whitaker, one of the most successful royal reporters of all time. James is not the Royal Family's favourite journalist, but then no one who takes royal reporting seriously ever is. Sycophancy has never produced a single royal story of any worth. James proved, with a series of exceptional revelations, that reporting on the Royal Family is a journalistic art form all its own. When James left the *Sun* to join the Express Group's new newspaper, the *Star*, I succeeded him in the royal seat. He remains a good friend, and an arch rival.

The other half of the royal team from the outset was *Sun* photographer, Arthur Edwards, the man who even more than James perfected the art of 'Charles following' and who laid the groundwork for the *Sun*'s world-exclusives.

James and Arthur were the team involved in the famous Prince-and-the-stag incident, a classic example, bordering on farce, of how best to annoy the Prince of Wales.

It happened in the summer of 1978, during the Royal Family's annual holiday at Balmoral, its Scottish estate. The Prince had spent a whole day stalking a stag, unaware that he in turn was being stalked by the *Sun* team. Arthur Edwards, hidden in the undergrowth, suddenly stood up to take a picture, startling the stag and sending it bounding off. As the Prince gave vent to his rage, the gillie accompanying him escorted the pair off the estate.

Arthur offered, apologetically: 'Will you tell His Royal Highness that, if it's any consolation, I've got a *picture* of the stag.' The gillie's answer is unprintable.

Arthur belongs to that rare breed, the true-born Cockney, gifted with a totally natural wit, a devouring capacity for sheer hard work and a keen eye for spotting the out-of-the-ordinary. He is also one of an even rarer breed: that of the photo-journalist, the photographer who does not wait to be told where to point his camera but who shares with the reporter the task of finding where the story is in the first place. Fleet Street possesses few such gems. Arthur is the brightest of them all.

His speech is hilariously colourful. His dropped 'aitches' are picked up for nobody. On the subject of taking pictures in focus, he would say: 'Getting 'em sharp is the easy part. It's getting the right girl in the frame that's 'ard.' And when the pressure was on to get a royal picture – any picture – in time for the first edition, his homespun wisdom produced the remark: 'Better a load of rubbish early than a Botticelli too late.'

In time, Arthur was to produce the Botticelli of them all.

Arthur has, above all else, an extraordinary ability to get on with everyone he meets and his cockney rhyming slang (which was, in time, picked up by every royal reporter in Fleet Street) is delivered to the whole world without apology. Prince Charles was no exception. From their first meeting an amazing repartee developed between the Prince and the photographer. It may have been that Prince Charles was so unaccustomed to being spoken to so freely by the man in the street that he welcomed Arthur's arrival like a breath of fresh air.

Or, as Arthur put it: 'I tell 'im what he's never heard before – the truth.'

The comment has some accuracy in that the Royal Family tend to be surrounded all their lives by those who are all too ready to agree with anything they say. The Queen, in particular, looks forward to off-the-record Press receptions because they are among the few occasions when she can find anyone to disagree with her. But while it could be argued that, to some members of the Royal Family, the world smells only of fresh paint and most of the globe's surface is covered with deep-pile red carpet, Prince Charles is more in touch with reality than any of his family. He meets, nevertheless, his share of sycophants, and a critic is a rarity.

On one occasion between chukkas at a polo match on Smiths Lawn, Windsor, a breathless Charles rode to the pony lines to change mounts, after scoring a spectacular goal.

'That was a good goal,' Arthur told him.

The Prince was startled. He looked up and said: 'That's very kind of you to say so, Mr Edwards. From you, that's compliment.'

Arthur checked himself. 'Mind you,' he said, 'if it'd been rubbish, I'd have told you so.'

The Prince laughed heartily and replied: 'I know you

49

would Mr Edwards, I know you would.'

One photograph which did not particularly please the Prince was taken as he lay asleep in the seat of his estate car at a polo match. The exclusive picture, taken by Arthur, showed a bald patch developing on the crown of his head. Sooner or later the patch would have been spotted by someone else, but the *Sun* was the first to tell its readers.

A few weeks later, Prince Charles walked up to Arthur and said, 'Ah, you are the man who took the picture of my bald patch. Luckily it only appeared in one newspaper. Have you many readers?'

'Only twelve million,' said Arthur.

The Prince groaned. 'Oh, God,' he said.

'Did you take a lot of stick over it?' Arthur asked.

'Well, people haven't said much to me,' said Prince Charles, 'but they keep trying to walk behind me to look at the back of my head.'

Then, looking at Arthur's rapidly thinning scalp, he said with a triumphant grin, 'You haven't so very much hair yourself.'

'No,' retorted Arthur, 'but you're a lot younger than me.'

The Prince decided he could not counter that point, and retreated from the fray.

Some time later, after we had both been away from home for several weeks, covering a Prince Charles tour, Arthur told him: 'If you don't get married soon, sir, my old woman's gonna divorce me and name you on the petition.'

'I'm doing my best,' said the beleaguered Prince, apologetically.

Charles genuinely takes as good as he gives in his exchanges – mainly good-natured – with the Press. But on many occasions he is the outright winner. He has to be, for no one is actually permitted to argue with him. The Prince occasionally takes advantage of this and will bawl out a Pressman, knowing his victim dare not shout back. To have a heated discussion with him is to court the risk of a formal complaint, and though the Prince may be in the wrong the outcome is unlikely to benefit the reporter or photographer.

A bawling-out from Prince Charles is an experience not easily forgotten.

During the early part of 1980, Arthur and I travelled to Sandringham to see who was the latest girl accompanying the Prince. Covering Sandringham, journalistically, is an immensely difficult task involving many hours of waiting around in the hope of chancing upon the Prince. No question, in royal situations, of walking up to the front door and making polite enquiries.

Early one morning as we were driving along a public lane on the Sandringham estate, a Range Rover flashed by us in the opposite direction. We had only a fleeting glimpse of the occupants.

'Who was in the front passenger seat?' demanded Arthur.

'A young woman with blonde hair, wearing a mauve-coloured blouse,' I replied. 'Why?'

''Cos the Prince of Wales was in the driving seat,' he said.

By pure chance, we had chosen to look at separate riders in the vehicle, and as we swiftly U-turned our car we resolved to adopt the same procedure in future. I would always look for the passenger, and Arthur the driver. By such arrangements can tiny advantages be gained.

The Range Rover lost us, and we did not find the royal vehicle again until lunchtime when it turned up at the village hall at Anmer, where the Royal Family often break off for lunch during shooting expeditions. The Prince was in a bad temper and, as we stood in the roadway outside the car, he stormed out of his vehicle, slammed the door hard enough to tear it from its hinges and gave me a dressing down in no uncertain terms for having the temerity to be there. I went rigid.

As the Prince disappeared into the hall, Arthur said calmly: 'The Prince of Wales was driving. Who was the passenger?'

'How the hell would I know?' I replied. 'It's very difficult to concentrate when you are getting a bollocking from the Prince of Wales.'

A few minutes later, Prince Charles came out of the hall

51

and happily posed for a photograph. The speed with which his moods change continues to amaze me. The girl, incidentally, we later identified as Patty Palmer-Tompkinson. Back to the drawing board.

After his purchase of Highgrove, the Prince was riding on his estate when he came across Arthur Edwards on a public footpath which crosses it.

'This is private property,' said the Prince, crossly.

'No, it's not,' said Arthur. 'It's a public right of way.' Charles disagreed. 'Look,' said Arthur, 'I'm not here to argue with you; go and look at the sign if you don't believe me.'

The Prince changed his angle of attack. 'Well, you shouldn't be taking pictures.'

'Why not?' retorted Arthur. 'It's my job.'

'Some job,' snapped Charles and galloped off towards the house. He stormed into the kitchen where a small group of police officers were sitting round a table drinking coffee. And in one of the rare situations where he had been known to swear, the red-faced Prince told them: 'You are supposed to be — well protecting me, and I've got Arthur Edwards on my front lawn!'

But it must be said, for the record, that for the great majority of the time, relations between the Prince and the Press are friendly. Only a few days after the Highgrove incident, Charles hailed Arthur with a friendly 'Hello, how are you?' as though it had never happened.

There were times when Prince Charles would positively go out of his way to give us a story and a picture. During a tour of an art gallery in Yugolsavia, he came across a painting of a beautiful girl – topless. He grinned and said to Arthur Edwards: 'Why don't you put her on Page Three?'

We did, of course, under the caption: 'By Royal Appointment.'

Photographers, through the very nature of their work, have to tread a wary path. Sometimes it is possible for a reporter to gather his information by telephone – but the photographer has to work in the front line. A necessary quality for the Fleet Street professional is to stand his ground when he knows he is in the right.

Prince Charles respects that professionalism, despite his occasional outbursts, and has never suffered an insult or an offensive remark. The Pressmen around him know their place, and try harder than he is aware not to step over the line. He is probably unaware too, that they have a great deal of sympathy with his position, and are monarchists to a man.

Prince Charles, though he has referred to 'the cruel accuracy of the camera lens', has also shown that he understands the difficulties they face. He once said: 'I look at it from the newspaperman's point of view: he's got a job to do – I've got a job to do. At times they happen to coincide, and compromise must occur, otherwise misery can so easily ensue. I try to put myself in their shoes, and I hope they try to put themselves in mine, although I appreciate that is difficult.'

There are some areas in which Prince Charles has a total misconception about the Press team attending him.

During a long flight to an overseas engagement, Charles and one of his detectives spent much of the journey discussing the hypothetical question of an attempt on the Prince's life. The Prince posed the question, which has often fascinated him: 'If someone came out of a crowd and tried to assassinate me and a photographer was nearby, would he shout a warning and try to come to my assistance, or would he take a photograph?' At the end of the debate, both men agreed that in such a situation he would take a photograph.

When I heard of the conversation, I put the same question in turn to all the photographers who cover his movements. Each one of them gave the same reply: 'I would go to his assistance. His life is more important than a picture.'

The fatal mistake in reporting on or photographing the Royal Family is to be afraid of them, to treat them as though they are unapproachable gods. They are, at the end of the day, human beings and have to be regarded as such.

The Prince once said: 'Unfortunately, the nicest people are those who won't come up and make themselves known. I think, good God what's wrong? Do I smell? Have I forgotten to change my socks? Then an awful lot of people eventually say: "Good Lord, you're not nearly as pompous as I thought you were going to be." So one has, in that sense, a lonely existence.'

Boldness can sometimes pay dividends. On one occasion when Prince Edward — Charles' youngest brother — was watching him at polo, Arthur tackled him on a story which had been doing the rounds.

According to gossip, Prince Edward had been flying to Balmoral on a scheduled aircraft when the captain's voice came over the tannoy to explain that the plane would have to divert because of fog at Aberdeen airport. The Prince, for whom the diversion meant a long and wearying journey by road, was said to have promptly left his seat and to have entered the flight deck, normally a forbidden area to passengers. There, he allegedly taxed the captain on the necessity for the diversion. Dissatisfied with the reply he received, the Prince, who normally travels on aircraft of the Queen's Flight, was said to have told the hapless captain, 'The RAF would have got me down', and returned to his seat. The story fits the rather unfair image Prince Edward has gained in recent years of being a surly, arrogant figure.

Arthur related the story to the Prince and asked if it were ture. Prince Edward laughed and explained that there was a factual basis to the account. His aircraft *had* been diverted, he *had* entered the flight deck, and he *had* asked why it was necessary. But, he went on, the captain had said that the aircraft did not have the same navigational equipment as a Royal Air Force plane and could not cope so well with thick fog.

'I assure you,' said the young Prince, 'I didn't say "The RAF would have got me down"!'

Arthur tapped his shoulder in a friendly gesture and told him: 'I'm glad you've told me that, 'cos I thought you were getting to be very flash.'

Prince Edward rocked with laughter at the typically East End remark, demonstrating that he is not the iceberg he is sometimes portrayed. Prince Edward, because of the little the public knows about him, is an enigmatic character. Hopefully, that exchange of confidence may pave the way to more examples of his humour in the future, and perhaps help us understand what goes through the mind of a young man who is third in line to the throne yet will never become king – except by a series of unthinkable accidents.

'Reporting on the Royal Family is the hardest job in Fleet Street,' the *Sun*'s former news editor, Ken Donlan, once said. 'No one wants to tell you anything.'

And so it remains. Buckingham Palace press office acts rather like a human brick wall, disseminating only the information it wishes to have known about the Royal Family. Any enquiry about the weekend plans of a Royal is certain to be met with the urbane comment: 'I'm sorry, but we couldn't possibly tell you that.'

The tracking of Prince Charle's love-life, therefore, required a different approach and, for me, the acquiring of a number of reliable contacts who could be depended upon to provide sound guidance and information. Arthur Edwards, with his bold approach, was invaluable in finding those contacts.

The situation also required constant vigilance.

It was not by chance, therefore, that we happened to be at the same polo match when Lady Diana Spencer turned up to watch the Prince, blushing deep red when Arthur spotted her. Her presence there was interesting because it was, in fact, her second meeting with the Prince that year.

It was never reported at the time, nor since, but in February 1980 Lady Diana was a guest of the Queen at Sandringham. Prince Charles barely noticed her – he has certainly never referred to that visit – because his companion that weekend was Amanda Knatchbull, the granddaughter of Lord Mountbatten. Lady Diana had gone along as a travelling companion.

Arthur was at Sandringham at the time, and received a tip that the two girls were travelling back together by train to Liverpool Street station, in London. Arthur had missed them when they set out from King's Lynn because he was diverted by a policeman waiting at the station to see them off. The officer, mistaking my colleague for a detective from London (his cameras were tucked away), told him: 'I've been told to watch out for a photographer called Arthur Edwards. He's a pretty smart character, apparently. If you spot him, will you let me know?'

'Of course I will,' promised Arthur.

I met the train in London with another photographer.

Normally it might have been difficult to spot the girls among the hundreds of passengers who poured off the train, and the platform has a dozen different exits. But the giveaway was their luggage. They had to wait for a trolley to carry the six or seven cases they were carrying. After loading up, Lady Diana spotted us waiting by the barrier and, nudging Amanda, went into a fit of giggles. Then, head down, she charged with the trolley for the taxi rank, sending the cases spinning all over the platform. The swift departure had gone slightly wrong, and she thanked us profusely while we picked up the cases.

The situation produced a useful set of photographs.

First Sandringham and then polo in Sussex . . . I began to wonder if there was something between this attractive blue-eyed blonde with an appealing sense of humour, and a Prince who was patently avoiding being seen with her.

Only time would tell. We could only wait and hope for another clue.

# Chapter Five

## Courtship

IT WAS without doubt, the most public wooing of the twentieth century. Part of it was the Prince's own doing – though through no fault of his own. Had he courted and proposed to a girl while in his early twenties he could have done so with far less publicity than he eventually received. But the older he grew, the more fascinated the general public became by his seemingly endless search for the right girl. It began to look as though he might remain a bachelor to the end of his days.

As it is, he is the only Prince of Wales to marry as late as his thirties since the 'Old Pretender' James Edward Stuart, who took a bride in 1718. The media, naturally, played its part in focusing attention on Charles, but for a little while the canny Prince managed to keep the budding romance a secret.

In July 1980, after the polo date, Lady Diana joined Prince Charles and the Royal Family on the Royal Yacht *Britannia* for the annual visit to the Isle of Wight for Cowes week. For the whole five days that she was aboard, she was not once glimpsed walking the decks. The great advantage of the royal yacht, as Charles has often remarked, is its built-in security, for no unauthorized person can board it and potential intruders can be spotted and warned away long before they become a serious threat. It seems, nevertheless, amazing that Lady Diana could have remained out of sight for so long, considering that, in Cowes harbour, the yacht is the focal point among the many thousands of small boats which sail around her.

The Royal Family are past masters at the art of diversion and, when one particular member wishes to avoid the public gaze, for one reason or another, a sister, brother or other relative takes on the task of playing 'decoy'. Thus when the

Prince and Lady Diana wanted to stay out of sight, brother Andrew 'drew the fire' by setting out in his own dinghy. Two boats, chartered by a posse of Pressmen, dutifully followed Prince Andrew who led them off to a quiet cove where he 'performed' for them by windsurfing for an hour or two.

The children of Princess Alexandra and the Hon. Angus Ogilvy, James and Marina, also played their part. They took off in a speedboat, with the royal policemen at the helm, in the opposite direction to Prince Andrew, thus splitting the Press forces and creating a double diversion. Later Prince Charles led the Press on a chase of his own, windsurfing and sailing in the harbour.

Presumably it was during these interludes that Lady Diana managed to go on deck for breaths of fresh air. No one will ever know because the week passed without a royal story of any significance getting into the newspapers and it was some considerable time before it was discovered that Lady Diana had been there at all. But Charles could not hope to hide the romance for much longer.

On Friday, 5 September 1980, Lady Diana left London to join Prince Charles and other members of the Royal Family, including the Queen, for a weekend at Balmoral, for the traditional Highland Games gathering. Diana had been to the Royal Family's Scottish home on several previous occasions but this weekend was different. The couple were beginning to realize that their happy relationship was developing into something stronger.

Arthur Edwards was there and secured his 'Botticelli' – exclusive pictures of the Prince fishing in the River Dee for salmon while Lady Diana watched him from the river bank. Inspiration, perhaps, produced the story which appeared in the *Sun* on the following Monday morning – inspiration aided by our exclusive knowledge of earlier dates between them.

I had one other useful guide: the observations of another guest that weekend at Balmoral who saw Charles and Diana together and remarked: 'She followed him around like a lamb.'

The *Sun*'s exclusive on 8 September appeared under the massive headline: 'He's in Love Again! Lady Di Is the New Girl for Charles.'

The story read:

> Prince Charles has found love on the rebound. After his broken romance with vivacious Anna Wallace, he has fallen head over heels for beautiful Lady Diana Spencer.
>
> She is nineteen and a perfect English rose. And last night friends were asking: 'Is it the real thing for Charles at last?'
>
> For dishy Diana is acceptable in every way to the Queen and Prince Philip. She is quiet-spoken, unassuming and has an impeccable background – the perfect qualities for a future Queen.
>
> The couple have just spent a discreet weekend together at Balmoral for the Highland Games. Lady Diana, sister of the Prince's old flame Lady Sarah Spencer, returned to London 'blissfully happy' last night.
>
> She and Charles went riding together on the Balmoral estate. And later, wearing waders and an old cap, Lady Diana watched from the banks of the River Dee as he fished for salmon.
>
> Whenever she was with Charles, her eyes never left him. A fellow guest at Balmoral told me:
>
> 'She is obviously captivated by the Prince. And Charles seems more happy and relaxed than I've seen him for a long time. Lady Diana obviously thinks the world of him – she never leaves his side unless told to stay in the background.
>
> 'She has around her all the aura of the Queen Mother, despite her youth. Everyone who meets her thinks she is wonderful.'
>
> In the past, Charles has favoured bubbly sophisticated girls-about-town. Now he may be ready to settle down with the more reserved Diana. Some observers

believe the Prince will follow a pattern, set by several Royals, of marrying a friend he can learn to love. Unlike some of Charles' previous girlfriends, Diana's background cannot be faulted.

Her father is the Earl Spencer, former equerry to the Queen. He is currently recovering from a stroke.

Her sister Jane is married to Robin Fellowes, the Queen's assistant private secretary. Diana's stepmother was unwilling to comment on the blossoming romance last night.

Lady Spencer said, 'I don't want to talk about it and neither does my husband.'

Many of the words in that story now have a prophetic ring to them, though at the time others in Fleet Street poured scorn on the report. Later, though, some newspapers claimed to have been the first to reveal the story of the romance, but nowhere can a cutting be found, dated before 8 September, telling of any such romance.

The 'blissfully happy' weekend over, Lady Diana returned to London, and to her work at the kindergarten, while Charles resumed his public engagements. Both felt excited, but unsure. Charles was to say later that it was in Balmoral that they both began to 'realize there was something in it'. But they did not discuss their feelings at the time, and could not be sure what was going through the other's mind.

A few day's after Diana's return, Charles sent the first symbol of his own feelings. Two dozen roses arrived at the flat in Old Brompton Road, hand-delivered from Buckingham Palace, and with a hand-written message from the Prince.

Secretly, Charles began to plan their next meeting. Again unknown to Fleet Street, Diana returned to Scotland to be near the Prince but, to avoid being detected, she stayed at Birkhall, the home of a romantic who acted as Cupid and a wise counsel as the romance blossomed in the soft Aberdeenshire air: the Queen Mother.

Lady Diana's departure from London and journey to

Scotland was planned – in the Prince's words – 'like a military operation', and this time Prince Charles and Lady Diana spent a weekend totally unobserved, walking and talking together, slowly testing out each other's feelings. It may well be that by now the die was cast, that the couple were so hopelessly entwined that there could only have been one final conclusion. But in royal affairs, such things are not so simple.

If anyone in Britain was still unaware of Prince Charles' romantic entanglement, they were put fully in the picture on 18 September when those revealing pictures of Lady Diana in a see-through skirt appeared in almost every national newspaper. Fleet Street had now begun to sit up and take notice of what the *Sun* had been saying, and a full force of photographers was waiting for a glimpse of the girl when she turned up for work at the Pimlico kindergarten.

So many inaccurate accounts have been written and spoken about how those sensational photographs were taken that it is time for the record to be put straight. Claims that Lady Diana was deliberately led into a trap, that photographers 'set her up', are totally untrue.

The truth is that it happened purely by chance. At the request of the photographers waiting outside, Lady Diana agreed to come out of the kindergarten and pose for pictures in the small park which stands alongside the nursery school. A particularly strong autumn sun was slanting down through the trees that morning as Lady Diana took up her position with a child in each arm to give the picture 'more interest'. As it turned out, the presence of the toddlers was superfluous. As Lady Diana stood with her legs just slightly apart, the photographers realized that the sun was shining through her skirt and that she had no petticoat underneath. It looked, for all the world, totally transparent. The technique of *'contre jour'* photography, with the light behind the subject, is well known to all serious photographers for the soft effect it gives to the face, and the glow around the hair. The see-through skirt was totally unexpected, and no one knew quite what to do about it. Certainly, no one knew quite how to tell Diana just how revealing she looked, and the Nikon motor-drives rattled like machine-guns.

That particular pose lasted for less than four minutes and photographers moved Lady Diana to several other positions – this time with the light in front of her – for further pictures. But it takes no guesswork to predict which particular snaps appealed to every picture editor in Fleet Street. The picture session also gave me my first opportunity to speak directly to the girl I had been writing about.

Without hesitation, the *Sun* splashed the picture and report the following day. Under the irreverent headline 'Charlie's Girl', it read:

> The bubbly blonde teenager tipped as the next Queen of England stepped regally into the limelight for the first time yesterday.
>
> Prince Charles' new girl, vivacious nineteen-year-old Lady Diana Spencer, posed for the photographers outside the kindergarten where she teaches. But she refused to speak about her romance with the Prince. And that silence improved her chances of making the marriage of the century. For the youngest daughter of the Earl of Spencer is the first serious girl-friend of the Prince who has kept mum.
>
> As I strolled with her through the grounds of the kindergarten, Lady Diana said:
>
> 'You know I cannot say anything about the Prince or my feelings for him. I am saying that off my own bat. No one has told me to stay quiet.'

A short while later, Diana was unable to stay quiet when she saw the picture that had been taken. Plainly she was horrified by the see-through effect of her cotton skirt, patterned with floral hearts.

Her deep embarrassment shone through as clearly as the sunlight when she said: 'I was so nervous about the whole thing I never thought I'd be standing with the light behind me.' She then added a comment which will go down in history as one of the most memorable spoken by the girl who will one day be queen: 'I don't want to be remembered for not having a petticoat.'

Prince Charles' press officer, Warwick Hutchins, added his own comment about the romance and, although it said nothing in itself, it was another clue to what lay ahead. He said: 'There is nothing I can say at the moment, but I cannot predict the future.' In other words: 'Wait and you will see.'

One aspect of that photographic session bothered all the royal writers in Fleet Street: was it possible that a girl who was to marry a king-to-be would happily pose for photographs 'like any other girl'? And would Buckingham Palace let her meet the Press without giving her some advice on how to cope with them. On the basis of those two puzzles alone, several writers dismissed her evermore from the running, to their own cost. But the questions *were* puzzling, and I put them to the only person who could provide the answers: Lady Diana.

She explained simply: 'I posed for the pictures because the photographers asked me politely, and they *had* been waiting outside for a long time.'

The answer may display naiveté, but it revealed, too, the kindness and consideration Diana has continued to extend to the Press ever since. As to the second question, Lady Diana assured me that she had received no coaching from Buckingham Palace, no advice to stay quiet, no contact at all. The reason was not difficult to find. Prince Charles had not dared to allow Buckingham Palace to intervene in the affair, or to speak on Diana's behalf because it would have been the first concrete sign that something was in the air.

It had never happened before with any previous girl-friend. Such a precedent would make it perfectly clear that Lady Diana was something special. Undoubtedly, however, Diana was already special. As the couple continued to meet secretly at the homes of their closest friends – the Parker-Bowles, the Tryons and others – Prince Charles treated the new lady in his life in a way he had never done before with all the other girls.

Diana often had to drive herself to see him, rather than be

collected, to avoid being seen, but Charles ensured that a police escort followed at a discreet distance to ensure her safety. In other ways, he was protective towards her. A married woman friend of Charles who observed him during this period told me:

> Prince Charles can be very cavalier in his attitude towards women. He often expects them to fend for themselves and I have known him to forget the normal courtesies that quite ordinary men remember, such as opening a car door for a lady. But with Lady Diana it was different. He was always attentive to her, and at dinner parties he would go out of his way to make sure that she was not left out of any conversation despite her shyness. Her happiness seemed to be the most important thing in his life.

Lady Diana was clearly now deeply in love with the Prince and, although she kept her silence in public, she spoke in private of 'my dear Charles'. She delighted everyone by backing Prince Charles when he rode his horse Allibar in an amateur riders' steeplechase at Ludlow Races in the October. But play-safe Di backed him for a place. She danced with excitement in the grandstand as the Prince, who had led for the first half of the three-mile chase but had slipped back to seventh place, fought to get back in the final furlong. He rode a hard finish to second place and collected £263 prize money while Diana picked up a third of the odds for the 10–1 bet. Afterwards all eyes were on the girl in a green overcoat and brown boots.

'It's marvellous,' said Lady Diana. 'He's worked really hard to get his weight down. He's only three pounds over his handicap.'

The Prince, though pleased at reaching second place, admitted, 'About halfway through the race, my concentration seemed to be distracted – and I had to work hard to get it back.' Di, as someone remarked later, could also be short for distraction.

The couple left the racecourse in separate cars and spent

*The Prince of Wales. A portrait.* PRESS ASSOCIATION

*The girl who nearly became queen. Lady Jane Wellesley with the Prince.* SUN

*'If he aske me I wou say no.' L Sarah Spencer Prince Charles. was she w introduce the Prince her youn; sister, La Diana.* SU

*The first date. Lady Diana watches Prince Charles at a polo match in Cowdray Park, July 1980.* SUN

*Lady Diana. A portrait.* SUN ▶

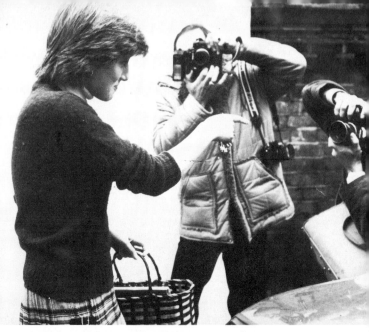

*Lady Diana is harassed by the Press.* SUN

*Balmoral, the weekend before the romance broke, 'when we began to think there was something in it.' Lady Diana dodges the cameramen.*
SUN ▶

*The famous photograph. 'I don't want to be remembered for having no petticoat.'* SUN

the weekend with the Parker-Bowles. On the Saturday, when he returned to the Wiltshire house at the end of a day's hunting, Diana could not contain her excitement at seeing Charles again – and ran down the drive to meet him.

Charles and Diana reached a major milestone in their growing romance early that November. The Queen gave her blessing to their partnership. Her formal consent would later be required for permission to marry, under the Royal Marriages Act of 1772 – so, too, would the consent of both Houses of Parliament. But that was still a long way off. The Queen had at this stage reached the conclusion that, if her son wished to marry Diana, it would be with her full support.

As the *Sun* put it: 'The Queen Says Yes to Diana.'

The Queen, who had known Diana since she was a baby, told her circle of intimates: 'She is a delightful girl. Charles could not find a more perfect partner.'

The pronouncement was crucial to the couple for, whatever their private thoughts, they both knew that the Queen's approval was essential before the question of marriage could even be considered. By making her own thoughts known, the Queen had at least put Charles' mind to rest. Lady Diana still did not know what the future held. They had not discussed marriage as such, and Charles was still hesitating. His self-doubts were understandable. He was a few days away from his thirty-second birthday. To have come this far in his life without making a major mistake, only to err in his most important decision of all would have been a folly of disastrous proportions. There was the age-gap, too.

Much later, Charles dismissed the twelve-and-a-half years between them as unimportant, but there is no doubt that in the early stages it taxed his mind considerably. He asked his trusted confidants their thoughts on the subject, and their unanimous verdict was that, if it did not worry the couple themselves, it would not matter to the nation at large. The worse that could happen, one predicted, is that it might produce a minor spate of comment about the difficulties couples sometimes face when there are ten years or more between their ages – but it was hardly a scandal. (When the time came, even those feared comments did not materialize.)

But Charles felt there was no royal marriage in recent history with which to compare his position, and he held back.

Rumours that an engagement announcement was imminent grew daily, particularly after the *Sun*'s exclusive story of the Queen's consent. Gossip columnist Nigel Dempster went to town on the *Sun* in his *Daily Mail* diary, pouring scorn on its reference to a possible engagement. Deliberately misquoting the *Sun*, he bet its editor £1000 that there would be no engagement announcement on Charles' thirty-second birthday. In fact, what the *Sun*'s second paragraph had said was: 'Friends of the couple predicted last night that the Prince *may* celebrate his thirty-second birthday on Friday by making an announcement about *his future* [my italics].'

Certainly options were left open. For one thing, there were reports that an announcement was imminent of the Prince's appointment as Governor-General of Australia. And it is true that there was a great deal of speculation among Charles' friends that he could not put off the question of Lady Diana much longer.

If Nigel Dempster was trying to tell his readers that an engagement would *never* take place then he got it all badly wrong. (He was still pressing the suit for Amanda Knatchbull at the time.) And if he was telling them that there *would* be an announcement but that he, Dempster, would be the first to reveal it, then his readers were in for a bitter disappointment. His silence, on the day after the announcement, was deafening. Instead, filled his column with trivia and even reproduced an old cutting headlined 'Lady Diana will be a May bride'.

On his thirty-second birthday (14 November) Prince Charles mounted another military operation to smuggle Diana into Sandringham for his party without anyone spotting her. Their weekend together left the Prince in a cheerful mood and he teased Pressmen who asked about an engagement date, as he set off for a stroll with his dog Harvey.

'You will all know what's happening in due course,' he

said, and when a photographer said: 'We rather hoped that Friday [his birthday] would be a rather special day for you,' he replied with a grin: 'So did everyone else.'

Lady Diana was given a police escort as she drove back to London, where a small but interesting development was noticed. Two policemen were patrolling the street below her flat. The protective arms of the Royal Family were beginning to close around her.

During this, the most difficult period of her life, Lady Diana's behaviour was exemplary, and she showed no little courage in dealing with the media men who were now calling at her flat daily. She blushed each time she was asked about Prince Charles, and the nickname 'Shy Di' began to stick. But she kept her vow never to use his name in conversation, or comment in any way about him. Lady Diana was already displaying the qualities needed for a future Queen. Not once was she rude to Pressmen, and many remember and admire her for it. A former Spencer family butler added fuel to the engagement rumours. Mr Ainslie Pendrey, who had retired at sixty-eight after serving the family for fifteen years, said: 'It's about time Charles made up his mind. I know he has escorted some lovely girls in his time, but none so beautiful as Lady Diana.' Mr Pendrey added an observation which was shared by others: 'The change in Lady Diana over the last six months has been remarkable. She has grown from a giggly schoolgirl into a beautiful and mature young woman.'

Mr Pendrey, who was known affectionately to the family as 'Pen', was able to throw fascinating light on the character of Lady Diana in her early teens. He recalled the night when she was given an unexpected dip in the private swimming pool.

'She and some of her girl-friends held a party and invited a rather lively group of boys,' he said. 'Towards the end of the evening – after everyone had got a little merry – some of the boys grabbed Lady Diana and threw her in the pool. But instead of getting out, Lady Diana threw off most of her clothes and swam around laughing.' It is just as well that Mr Pendrey ended the story by saying: 'It was all innocent fun.

She asked for her bikini and put it on before she got out.'

But just in case his account of the prank left doubt in anyone's mind, Diana's stepgrandmother, Barbara Cartland, cooed sweetly the next day: 'She is purity itself.'

Lady Diana also scored a notable 'first' over any of her rivals early in November 1980. She was given a tour of Highgrove, the Prince's new home. Charles personally escorted her over the house and she listened while he enthusiastically outlined his plans for its renovation and décor.

The West Country hostess who entertained the couple on that visit said at the time, 'I wouldn't be surprised if she is helping to choose the curtains.' She reflected the mood of the nation when she added: 'Sometimes I give up hope of him ever popping the question. The longer he is a bachelor, the more indecisive he becomes.' More hopefully, she commented: 'If looks are anything to go by, they are made for each other. And Charles is acting like a teenager again.'

Diana took another significant step forward on 4 November when she was invited by Charles to Princess Margaret's fiftieth birthday party at London's Ritz, an opportunity for her to meet the assembled Royal Family – including the Queen, Prince Philip, Princess Anne and her husband, the Queen Mother and Princess Margaret's children. And it meant, too, that she was now welcome within the Royal Family's inner circle. She arrived quietly, looking beautiful in a peach-coloured evening gown and fur stole, and slipped into the hotel unnoticed through a side door. Once again, Charles and Diana left separately, at the end of the party, determined not to be seen together as a couple.

It is fair to say, that, as November drew to a close, Prince Charles was beginning to fall into a trap of his own creation. It is difficult to see how he could have broken off the romance without the biggest royal storm in years. Above all else, the humiliation for Lady Diana would have been heartbreaking. True, Charles had broken off many romances in the past but never before with a girl he had brought this far 'down the garden path'. Without issuing any official denials of a romance through Buckingham Palace Press office, he could have asked the staff there to gently guide the Press, by way of off-the-record guidance, to 'cool things' and steer them from talk of marriage. But he said and did nothing.

Even cautious Charles was beginning to realize that he could not sit on the fence for ever. His difficulties were not assisted by the fact that the pressures on Lady Diana were now becoming distressing.

Overseas newspapers and magazines, sensing from the British Press that here at last was the girl for the dashing heir to the throne, sent their own staffmen to view the situation. Among the small army which camped outside Lady Diana's flat were the Italian photographers, the *paparazzi* so hated by the British Royal Family. Their ruthlessness in obtaining pictures, whatever the pain to others, is notorious throughout Europe. After Prince Charles' first experience of them, he remarked to British photographers: 'It makes me realize what gentlemen you all are.'

(After the engagement announcement, there was an attempt to break into Lady Diana's flat, and thieves succeeded in getting into her mother's home. Police enquiries are still continuing at the time of writing, but Fleet Street men have their own thoughts, particularly as the only item stolen from Diana's mother's home was a photograph album containing old family snapshots.)

The *paparazzi* brought havoc to the kindergarten where one photographer pushed his camera through a back window and set off a flash. (Such behaviour would bring instant dismissal for a British newspaperman.) Lady Diana was followed everywhere she went and, with the help of her flatmates, a complicated game of 'Find the Lady' was devised. Her distinctive Mini Metro would be moved around and parked in all sorts of odd places at unusual times. And while the girls acted as decoys, Diana would slip out the back entrance and take a taxi to meet the Prince, or be picked up by a royal car.

Only once did Lady Diana break down under the pressure.

A group of Continental photographers followed her during a shopping expedition in Oxford Street, and created such embarrassing scenes that finally she burst into tears.

A short while after the incident, Arthur Edwards and I held a long conversation with Diana on the doorstep of her flat about the pressures she faced. Arthur felt shame for his overseas counterparts. And he delivered some fatherly advice to a girl who, despite her high-born connections, was facing her problem alone.

'Listen, love,' he said, with genuine concern. 'You are better than them. You just hold your head up, and remember who you are. Don't let 'em make you break down again.'

Lady Diana, looking more vulnerable than ever, was doubtful. Arthur went on: 'I'll tell you something else. I've met all Prince Charles' girlfriends, and you're streets ahead of all of 'em. If he doesn't marry you, he's out of his tiny mind.' Lady Diana cheered up immediately, and smiled in gratitude.

'Oh, and one more thing,' added Arthur. 'Don't forget when it's "Your Majesty" for you, its "Sir Arthur" for me.'

As Prince Charles has done so many times before, Lady Diana roared her head off at Arthur's joke. But I think the advice did some good as well. For she never broke down under the stress created by unscrupulous photographers.

The story of Prince Charles and Lady Diana's courtship is, sadly, not complete without a reference to 'That Royal Train Story'. The allegation that Lady Diana and Prince Charles spent several hours together, for two nights in succession, in a carriage of the royal train, was an unnecessary blight on the couple's happiness. And it caused a rift between the Queen and Fleet Street which will take some considerable time to completely heal.

The allegation was made by the *Sunday Mirror* and, with its references to Lady Diana staying with the Prince 'until the early hours', it contained unmistakeable innuendoes. The meetings were said to have taken place on the nights of 5 and 6 November as the train stood in what the newspaper referred to as a 'secluded siding' during a West Country tour.

The *Sunday People* compounded the original story's felony by 'lifting' it for its later editions – without checking it – under the suggestive headline 'Di's Love Dates on Royal Train'.

The Queen was furious at the reports, and her Press secretary, Mr Michael Shea, wrote to the *Sunday Mirror*'s editor demanding a retraction. It was an unprecedented move by the Palace and Mr Shea made clear the Queen's views when he said, 'This is a forceful demand. To suggest that the Prince of Wales used the royal train for the sort of thing that is the clear innuendo in the paper caused offence – and rightly so and is completely untrue.' Mr Shea went on:

> Prince Charles was on the royal train on the nights in question. On the first occasion he had three guests on board – the secretary of the Duchy of Cornwall, his successor and the local land steward and they were discussing the Duchy of Cornwall estate.
>
> On the other occasion, the train stopped there between two and five in the morning and there was no question of anyone coming aboard. It was quite absurd to suggest that anyone could be smuggled aboard.

Mr Shea, in his letter to the *Sunday Mirror* editor, said that 'grave exception' had been taken to the story, and he sought an apology. In its following edition, the *Sunday Mirror* did not apologise but published, with the agreement of Mr Shea, their exchange of correspondence. In the days which followed, the Palace considered reporting the matter to the Press Council, the body which adjudicates in complaints against Fleet Street, but the matter was allowed to drop.

The Queen and Prince Charles were bitter about the refusal to apologize, and their anger over the story continued for some time. For it not only placed Lady Diana in a tawdry light, but it effectively accused Prince Charles of using the taxpayers' money (i.e., the royal train) for his own private purposes. The Queen's intervention was seen by the rest of Fleet Street as a sure sign that there *was* something special in the relationship between Prince Charles and Lady Diana, and she was criticized for increasing the pressures for an announcement. But in the circumstances, there was little else the Queen could have done. The publication of the story naturally led to enquiries of the Palace Press office by other newspapers. And to have issued a 'No comment' would instantly have been read as confirmation.

The fault, in many people's eyes, lay with the *Sunday Mirror*'s refusal to apologize. Anyone can make a mistake, and it is accepted that the story was printed in good faith. But once the denial had been issued, on the Queen's specific instructions, it must have been obvious to the newspaper that it had got it wrong. The answer at that stage was a straightforward retraction and an apology. Other editors have faced up to mistakes on many previous occasions and backed down with dignity. The *Sunday Mirror* were left looking foolishly stubborn and childishly petulant. They described their source for the story as 'impeccable' without, naturally, naming him. In fact the source is known to most Fleet Street editors, news editors and royal writers, and to describe him as 'impeccable' is an exaggeration to say the very least. I personally investigated the allegations and it took a remarkably short time to establish that they were totally untrue.

Lady Diana denied them herself. Having kept her silence on other matters for many months, she said: 'I stayed in that evening with my flatmates. That is the absolute truth. I had some supper and watched TV before going to bed early.' She went further: 'I was not on the royal train when they said and have never been on the royal train. I don't even know what it looks like.'

That should have been enough. The *Sunday Mirror* were wrong and Fleet Street's reputation was left the poorer by their failure to face up to it.

If there was nothing Prince Charles could immediately do to help Lady Diana in her predicament, he tried to make up for it by becoming a faithful suitor to her. Throughout his bachelorhood, he had been a notorious 'two-timer'; while apparently squiring one young lady, there would always be another waiting on the end of a telephone. He revelled in his ability to pick up and drop girls at will, and few ever complained. To share just one evening with the heir to the throne was enough for a girl to become celebrated. Her company would be sought ever after by a whole queue of eligible young men and several ex-girl-friends of the Prince married soon after their dalliance with Charles was over. The girl-friends of these girls would be green with envy. Never was the old music hall song so appropriate: 'I've danced with a man, who's danced with a girl who's danced with the Prince of Wales.'

A member of Prince Charles' staff at the time told me: 'He always liked to have another string to his bow. The girls seemed to think he was faithful to each of them in turn, but in fact he was often seeing two at a time.' Thus when Charles' name was being publicly linked with banker's daughter Sabrina Guinness, he was also secretly dating dark-haired Jane Bonham-Carter, the twenty-two-year-old daughter of former leading Liberal Mark Bonham-Carter.

Some of the girls did discover what was going on, however, and gave up Charles because they objected to being cheated 'on the side'. Even the girl-friend of a Crown Prince has her pride.

But if the Prince of Wales ever possessed a 'little black book' it was at about this time that he destroyed it. For he gave up his 'double-dating' lifestyle and remained true to Diana. At weekends, when he was not with Diana, Charles became obsessive about not being seen with any other girl. A photograph of him talking to another young lady – however innocent the relationship – could have been misinterpreted. He was at pains not to hurt Lady Diana's feelings, and it may also have been going through the Prince's mind that, if the romance did lead to marriage, he wanted history to show that the courtship had been unblemished.

Even Charles began to see the funny side of the suspense that the Press and the nation felt at the time. At a reception at London's Savoy Hotel, he looked up in mock puzzlement at the glaring lights of the television crews who had joined the phalanx of photographers now following him everywhere – 'just in case'.

The amused Prince told his audience: 'I can't think what useful information to impart on an occasion like this. But, judging by the brightness of the lights, somebody must think I have something to say.'

Behind the scenes the Prince began to make discreet enquiries about the possibilities and implications of marriage to Lady Diana. He discovered that the age-gap, far from being a liability, was positively welcomed by advisers to the Royal Family. He could marry at whatever age he wished but, for gynaecological reasons, his bride should be in her early twenties – the ideal age for bearing children. To take a bride nearer his own age, advisers agreed, would be a gamble he could not afford. The wife of the man who will be king must, above all else, become a mother and ensure the succession. It requires no elaboration here to say that for an heir to the throne to take a wife and *afterwards* find out that she was incapable of bearing children would be an elementary mistake the Royal Family would never make.

It is also standard procedure in the Royal Family that, when a prince or princess falls in love and wishes to marry, a 'cooling off' break is arranged. The couple are parted, usually by an overseas trip for one of them, to give both the opportunity of carefully considering the enormous step each was preparing to take, without the distraction of the other's presence. The old adage which says that 'absence makes the heart grow fonder' may often be true, but it can also serve to bring a young lover to his or her senses and realize that what seemed a deep and lasting love was, after all, only infatuation. It was felt that Charles was old enough to know his own mind, but Lady Diana was after all only nineteen. She too must be given the chance of considering what she was letting herself in for. The Queen Mother was pressing, in her gentle way, that the couple should not 'rush things'. In the case of Charles and Diana, there was no need to artificially arrange a 'testing time', for the Prince was already

74

scheduled to make a trip overseas – an official visit planned many months before – to the land of Princes and poverty – India.

Lady Diana must have felt very much 'left behind' as her Prince flew off to the sub-continent 4000 miles away. But it might have been some consolation had she known that she was the only girl he said goodbye to.

There would scarcely have been time for him to say 'farewell my lovely' to all the girls he had known. But there were many who must have known that their chances of walking down the aisle with the heir to the throne were gone for ever.

# Chapter Six

## The Girls He Left Behind

THE POPULAR newspapers called them 'Charlie's Angels' after the American television show. 'Charlie's Darlings' was another version, while the Prince's bodyguards could sometimes be heard referring to them, under their breaths, as simply 'a bloody nuisance', for they brought more complications into the life of the Prince of Wales, and his accompanying policemen, than all his official engagements put together.

Prince Charles, when he is a happily married man with his children around him, will never be able to say that he didn't 'play the field'. He played acres of them.

'The trouble with Charles is that he falls in love very easily,' one of his girl-friends remarked. If that was true he fell *out* of love just as easily. Winsome beauties fluttered in and out of his life like butterflies. And as quickly as one ended its brief span in the bright light, so another chrysalis was opening up.

They came in all shapes, sizes and nationalities – all of them beautiful – but it is difficult to see how more than a handful measured up to the standards Prince Charles had set for himself. For he was fond of waxing long and lyrical about 'the girl that I'll marry'. Her qualities were so wide and wonderful that one doubted such a creature existed, until Lady Diana came along. Before then she was a figment of a romantic's imagination.

'When you marry in my position,' he once remarked, 'you are going to marry someone who perhaps one day is going to become Queen. You have got to choose somebody very carefully, I think, who could fulfil this particular role and it has got to be someone pretty special. The one advantage about marrying a princess, for instance, or somebody from a royal family, is that they do know what happens.' It is a fact of life that as Charles grew older, princesses became pretty thin on the ground, particularly virginal ones. And it was a necessary criterion from the start that a bride for Charles had to be lily-white.

Several fell by the wayside when it was discovered they had a 'past' – a 'track record' as the punters say. Others were no more than names drawn out of a hat by the gossip columnists and were never serious propositions in the first place. Others came close to marrying the Prince.

An arranged marriage has never been a threat to Charles. He was given his head, and allowed to choose for himself – mistakes and all. 'I shall marry for love,' he said early on, but his ideas changed as he matured. His father made it clear many years ago that he had never specified the sort of girl Charles should marry – 'not even a princess'. He explained: 'You will find that people tend to marry within their own circle . . . The advantage perhaps is that there is a certain built-in acceptance of the sort of life you are going to lead.' Prince Charles echoed that comment when he said: 'She's got to have some knowledge of the job, some sense of it. Otherwise she wouldn't have a clue about whether she is going to like it.'

Drawing up a list of eligible 'hopefuls' has long been a favourite game of British newspapers, and if none of them ever succeeded in finding the correct one, they perhaps saved the Prince the chore of reading through *Burke's Peerage* or *Debrett's*. The first of these lists contained three princesses, two Earl's daughters and a whole motley of lesser blue-bloods. Charles was then just four years old. In another year the list of possibles included *Princess Marie-Christine of the Netherlands, Princess Anne Marie of Denmark,* the sisters *Lady Caroline Percy, Lady Victoria Percy* and *Lady Julia Percy,* and *Lady Georgina Petty-FitzMaurice.* Charles was too busy to study the list himself; he was enjoying his eleventh birthday party at Buckingham Palace.

The Prince of Wales approached his courting days with not inconsiderable trepidation. The public eye would be upon him from his very first date. For this reason, Prince Charles was a 'late starter' (some might say that he made up for that in the fulness of time). He had the inevitable teenage crushes. They started at fourteen, when he treated his second cousin Marilyn Wills to a thirty-bob seat in the stalls to see *The Sound of Music*. If her voice was music to his ears, it didn't last long. Next came Sandra Spence – the first of many blondes in his life – the solicitor's daughter in Elgin, Scotland, who invited half a dozen boys from Gordonstoun School – including the gangling seventeen-year-old Charles – to join several girls for her birthday party.

'There was no necking,' Miss Spence explained later, partly for her father's benefit. 'We were all in one room, and the Prince's detective was there all the time.' In fact Charles and Sandra hardly spoke at the party. He spent most of the evening making 'small talk' with a local farmer's daughter. But his name was inevitably linked with Sandra's and when he left, shortly afterwards, to continue his schooling at Timbertop in Australia, he earned himself the headline in a Continental newspaper: 'Exiled for the Crime of Falling in Love'.

The Prince learned, too, in his schooldays that the most innocent of exchanges with a girl of about his own age, was likely to court gossip and innuendo. While at Timbertop, he received a friendly – almost 'pen pal' – letter from *Rosaleen Bagge*, the daughter of a Sandringham neighbour. Rosaleen will go down in history as one of the first girls he ever held in his arms – he had danced with her at a country house ball in Norfolk, the previous winter. The Prince, somewhat lonely in his new 'Aussie' surroundings, was grateful for another contact with home and wrote an equally friendly reply. News of the 'romance' leaked out and Rosaleen – about as unlikely to become his bride as American film actress Farrah Fawcett, whom he met many years later – was added to the list of contenders for the throne.

Charles learned his lesson and became more discreet in his contacts with the opposite sex. Several years passed without another girl's name cropping up. And for all the girls who were to touch his life, Charles never had anything of the rake about him. Not for him the philandering of that other Prince of Wales, his great-great-grandfather who became Edward VII.

Charles was nineteen and a student at Cambridge when he met the girl universally accepted as the first love of his life. She was *Lucia Santa Cruz*, the daughter of the then Chilean Ambassador to London, and a tasty Latin American dish by anyone's standards. Their first meeting coincided with a startling discovery Charles had made. All his life, he had been brought up with the understanding that 'nice' girls only slept with boys after marriage. In the Victorian atmosphere of his nurseries, he believed that girls who did share their boyfriends' beds were, in the colloquialism of that era, 'tarts'. At Cambridge he found that intelligent, well-educated girls who didn't seem like tarts at all were hopping in and out of beds like nobody's business. The discovery opened up a whole new chapter for the impressionable Prince.

His attempts to find a paragon of virtue for a wife were, he found, somewhat confounded by the relaxed attitudes of the 'Swinging Sixties' with its new moralities, and bra-burning women's lib movement. Girls took lovers as easily as men.

Suggestions by distinguished author and former colleague, Anthony Holden, that Lucia and Charles went beyond the kissing and cuddling stage sparked off a right royal row in 1979. According to Holden, in his book, *Charles, Prince of Wales,* the undergraduate was 'wholly inexperienced', while the lovely Lucia was three years older, 'vivacious and considerably more experienced in the ways of the world'.

Further, he suggested that Lord 'Rab' Butler, then Master of Trinity College, 'slipped a key' to the college to Lucia so that she could be alone with Charles. Lord Butler, said Holden, 'felt it his duty to help Prince Charles enjoy the dwindling days of as private a life as he would ever know'. The former Tory minister hotly denied the allegation, pointing out that he never had any college keys to 'slip'. But the author countered by producing a letter in Lord Butler's own handwriting which said: 'At the Prince's request, my wife and I allowed Lucia to stay in the Master's Lodge so that they could have more privacy.'

Lucia, herself, kept her silence on the subject. Asked if she had enjoyed a date with Charles, she said in an accent straight out of *West Side Story*: 'You may assume I deed.' But when asked if she and Charles were in love, she declared: 'I no longer speak Eenglish.'

Whatever the truth of those long-off varsity days, Prince Charles was never without a girl on his arm after that, reflecting an old saying that when a young man discovers sex, he feels for some time as though he's invented it!

Lucia eventually married a Chilean lawyer and Charles, although he missed their wedding, was godfather to their first child. Charles, still at Cambridge, turned his attention to *Sibella Dorman*, daughter of the Governor-General of Malta, Sir Maurice Dorman. She joined the Prince for a private dinner and was a guest aboard the Royal yacht for the celebration which followed his investiture as Prince of Wales in 1969.

Journalists, who followed them to Malta where they holidayed in the sun, couldn't believe their eyes as they watched her gently rubbing suntan oil into his skin. Sibella, legend now has it, climbed the walls of Newham College after a late night date with the Prince left her locked out.

But, like many after her, the Governor-General's daughter moved on – and so did Charles. His thoughts began to change as he realized that his quest for a bride was not going to be the relatively straightforward affair he'd thought it might be. 'I think you are very lucky if you find the person attractive in the physical and mental sense,' he said.

When Charles was twenty-three, a clumsy attempt was made to match him with *Princess Caroline of Monaco*, the wayward daughter of Prince Rainier and the former American movie star of *High Society* fame, Grace Kelly. Their meeting, during a visit by the Prince to France, seems to have been arranged for no other reason than she *was* a princess, but their brief encounter was a disaster. Caroline, then only fifteen, displayed her attitude to the match-making by arriving an hour late for their date and was as embarrassed as the Prince. After a series of polite exchanges, they parted and never met again.

Charles summed it up: 'Before I arrived, the world had me engaged to Caroline. With our first meeting the world had us married – and now the marriage is in trouble.'

A similar fate befell an attempt to pair off the Prince with *Tricia Nixon,* daughter of American President Richard Nixon, during a visit to the White House. Charles became irritated by awkward manoeuvres to bring the two of them together, particularly when the President told him, with the subtlety of a blunderbuss: 'My wife and I will keep out of the way so you can really feel at home.'

Charles was angry enough to dismiss Tricia as 'artificial and plastic', though he did concede that her sister Julie had a 'bright, warm personality'. Nixon, who was never noted for his judgement – his Watergate Waterloo lay ahead – possibly pushed the wrong daughter.

Prince Charles found it better, after that experience, to learn from his own mistakes and choose his own girls. 'Whatever your place in life,' he said, 'when you marry you are forming a partnership which you hope will last for fifty years. So I'd want to marry someone who had interests I could share. If I'm deciding on whom I want to live with for fifty years – well, that's the last decision on which I would want my head to be ruled entirely by my heart.'

The heart had its way, however, for many more flings. In time, his name was linked with no fewer than sixty-four eligible girls, twenty of them princesses. They included:

*Bettina Lindsay.* Charles became 'very fond' of Bettina, Lord Balniel's daughter. Then a flaxen-haired twenty-one-year-old, she met Prince Charles at the home of the Marquess of Salisbury and was invited to stay at Balmoral and Windsor as well as invited to go to the theatre and a concert at the Albert Hall. At first her qualifications seemed perfect. Her grandfather was the Earl of Crawford and

Balcarres, the premier Earl of Scotland, and she spoke fluent French, German, Italian and Russian. But she favoured way-out clothes, including outrageous hats, and admitted that after a year studying in Paris she enjoyed 'living like a Beatnik'. Beatniks do not become Queens.

*Countess Angelika Lazensky,* a Czech beauty, described her four-day stay at Balmoral as 'blissful'. She went further: 'The Prince,' she said, 'is without exception the most wonderful, charming person I have ever met. But whether he loves me or not, I cannot say. You will have to ask him what is in his heart.' That ended the romance. Angelika had broken the royal golden rule of 'never kiss and tell'.

*Fiona Watson,* the daughter of Yorkshire landowner Lord Manton, made a sensational exit. The Prince had no sooner met her and decided he liked her than it was learned that her 38–23–35 charms had been displayed in glorious colour across seven pages of the 'girlie' magazine *Penthouse*. The Prince never quite recovered from the shock.

*Laura Jo Watkins* was a blonde, beautiful, all-American package, complete with pouting lips, and for a while Charles thought her 'wonderful'. They met at a yacht club in California in 1975, when the Prince's ship *Jupiter* made a courtesy call on San Diego. She flew to London at his suggestion and royal approval seemed to have been given when she popped up in the Strangers' Gallery of the House of Lords to listen to the Prince's maiden speech. But Charles soon tired of her, and she returned, crestfallen, to America. She made a brief reappearance the following year, when Charles travelled to France for his traditional 'high-life' weekend at Deauville. The Prince's polo-playing friend Guy Wildenstein flew Laura to Deauville for a reunion. But Charles was embarrassed, rather than pleased, by the 'surprise present' and the whole thing fizzled out.

*Sabrina Guinness,* the effervescent brewery heiress, fascinated Charles, but not so much that he resisted dating other girls without her knowledge. Once he showed a taste for a double Guinness by taking Sabrina and her equally delicious twin Miranda, then twenty-four, to a glittering black-tie-and-tiara ball at the Earl of Pembroke's stately home, near Salisbury, Wiltshire. He danced the night away, amid a hubbub over the champagne that he was about to make a dramatic announcement. But he left alone at 4.00 a.m. – leaving no one the wiser.

*Susan George,* the actress, also made a brief appearance and was a special guest at his thirtieth birthday party. She was among a handful in his life who regularly kissed him on the cheek on greeting him. Charles had a definite soft spot for her but she was more an indulgence he allowed himself than a true love.

*Jane Ward* emerged from her friendship with Charles a heartbroken figure. She is still 'listed' by journalists as one of his past loves but the truth is that Jane, a blonde divorcée, was never ever a girl-friend in the accepted sense. Her life was shattered in the summer of 1979 when she was working as assistant manager of the Guards Polo Club, where the Prince played. A rumour swept Fleet Street that 'the William Hickey Diary' in the *Daily Express* was about to reveal a story of the Queen's 'concern' at the friendship between Jane and Charles.

On the evening before the story broke, I went to Windsor to interview Jane so that the *Sun* would have a story in time for the *Express* first edition. James Whitaker of the *Star* arrived almost simultaneously and together we spoke to Jane, over a shared bottle of wine. She admitted that the Queen had always been cool to her 'although she has nothing to worry about'. Jane saw her friendship for what it was. She explained: 'Prince Charles and I both know that there could never be anything between us, that nothing could come of our friendship because I am a divorcée. We both accept the situation.'

That might have been the end of it but Jane began to open up her heart. 'Sometimes I think it could have been different had I never been married. But there it is – we both accept life as it is. Charles is a lonely guy and he loves to flirt. We tease each other and once he kissed and hugged me – but it was all in fun.' Blue-eyed Jane, who had been divorced only a few months earlier from Royal Hussars officer Toby Ward, was honest enough to add: 'Nothing will ever come of our friendship. As to marriage – that's laughable.'

An honest girl speaking her mind. But the damage was done, and the following morning's headlines – including 'My Friend Charles, by Jane' – put the cat among the pigeons. At the height of the furore, Jane turned up to watch Charles play polo at Cowdray Park, Sussex, the following weekend. She had hoped to have a word with the Prince but she was approached by Chief Inspector John MacLean; they spoke for a few moments and she left the ground, in tears. She told me as she drove off: 'I haven't spoken to the Prince. I may never see him again.'

A few weeks later Jane left England for South America to produce a film about polo and, to my knowledge, has not returned. The abrupt end of her friendship with Charles is one of the unhappiest chapters in her life and it must be said that the Press played its part in bringing it all about. But we shall never know just how 'concerned' the Queen was and why Charles let her scurry out of his life without so much as a goodbye. The one fact is that she had embarrassed the Royal Family, and for poor Jane there was no going back.

She is now just a footnote in royal history, but in her time reached a far better perception of what made Prince Charles tick than any of the 'young things' who briefly entered his life. During that frank summer's evening interview she told me:

He relaxes in my company because I don't treat him as untouchable. I sometimes think that he likes me because I am honest and open with him. And perhaps he feels safe in my company because I am a divorcée and he knows we could never be married. He has a very strong sense of duty and he is a very moral person. It worries him that so many of his friends have been divorced. I am sure it has put him off marriage because he has certainly become wary. I'm sure he would like to marry but he hasn't met the right girl yet.

A perceptive girl, indeed.

*Amanda Knatchbull* had a curious dalliance with the Prince. She came into the picture in November 1979, following the death of her grandfather Lord Mountbatten. The Prince had known her since she was a baby and, as related earlier, 'Uncle Dickie' had urged him to consider Amanda or her sister Joanna as a potential bride. It was a wish close to Earl Mountbatten's heart and when he died Charles – perhaps out of respect – did 'consider' the girls. He spent a weekend at their family home in the village of Mersham, Kent. It was natural enough for him to visit the house – he had been a friend of the girls and their parents, Lord and Lady Brabourne, for some years – but coming so soon after the death of the Earl, its timing was significant. Both granddaughters have haughty aristocratic looks and a first-class pedigree. Though it is thought he favoured Amanda, a romance never got off the ground.

Certainly the visit did nothing for his mood. Armed police arrived to guard the cottage in the Kentish countryside where he lunched with the girls, after Arthur Edwards and I arrived following a tip-off. And although we did not stray from the public road, difficulties with the police approached harassment. Elaborate precautions were taken to prevent photographs being taken and, when the weekend was over, Charles went back to London and did not return. Amanda was consigned to the long list of girls who might have been.

The sojourn in Kent was an unusually unhappy one for the Prince, for he otherwise managed to maintain his sense of humour throughout his search for a likely lass. During a tour of Australia he took it all in good part when shapely, bikini-clad Jane Priest ran up to him, as he surfed in the sea off a Perth beach, and planted a kiss on the royal lips. He went so far as to hold her in a clinch for a few seconds even though he knew the 'spontaneous' situation had been set up by photographers desperate for a good picture. And later when an admirer in the Perth crowd called out, 'When are you going to get married then?' he replied with a laugh: 'I only wish I knew.'

During another tour, this time on safari in Kenya, he was rumoured to be in the company of a 'mystery blonde'. He eventually emerged from the bush and handed *Sun* reporter Iain Walker a home-made stuffed bird, complete with blonde wig and a label around its neck with the words 'mystery bird'. 'Is this the blonde bird you are looking for?' he asked with a grin.

There were some girls who mattered more than others.

*Lady Sarah Spencer,* sister of Lady Diana, was at one stage a serious contender for marriage. She joined the Prince as his skiing companion when he travelled with the Duke and Duchess of Gloucester to Klosters in February 1978. The Prince had, once again, known her since childhood but it seemed at least a compliment – if not significant – that he had selected Sarah, a stunning redhead, to accompany him. The trip was the first of what has now become an annual winter sports holiday with the Palmer-Tompkinsons in their tiny chalet.

Lady Sarah had a wonderful time, even though she occasionally had difficulty in keeping up with the other skiers and she fell frequently. But her real tumble – from grace – was the result of a familiar failing: talking about the Prince. In the relaxed atmosphere of the mountain village, it was possible for a journalist to go up to the front door of the chalet to make an enquiry. One enterprising reporter did just that, and Lady Sarah gave him an interview on the doorstep. As she spoke, Prince Charles went by with only a towel wrapped round him, on his way to the shower, and remarked pleasantly: 'Don't mind me.'

Lady Sarah revealed that she had once suffered from anorexia nervosa, the so-called 'slimmers disease' and had nearly died. If that wasn't startling enough, she went on to speak her mind about the Prince. 'Charles is a fabulous person,' she said 'but I am not in love with him. He is a romantic who falls in love easily. I can assure you that, if there were to be an engagement between Prince Charles and myself, it would have happened by now.'

Lady Sarah saved the barb for the end: 'I would not marry

a man I did not love, whether it was a dustman or the King of England. If he asked me, I would turn him down.'

When the story hit London, Charles was deeply hurt. To be compared with a dustman was bad enough, but to have your affection thrown in your face before any serious romance had a chance to develop was too much. Exit Sarah.

She was not the only one, however, to give the Prince of Wales a taste of his own medicine.

*Anna Wallace* gave Charles the royal 'brush-off' in no uncertain terms. Anna, another blonde, twenty-five years old, daughter of a Scottish landowner, Hamish Wallace, was working as a secretary in London when she met Charles at a hunt in the autumn of 1979. Anna – nicknamed 'whiplash' because, it is said, of her love for hunting – has the reputation of a fiery temper. But they seemed to hit it off together and dated for nearly a year. Charles is thought to have actually proposed to her in the spring of 1980, but whatever her reply the affair ended abruptly – and in style.

It was the night of 1 August 1980, and the Prince had taken Anna as his partner for the evening to Windsor Castle where an elaborate ball had been arranged in honour of the Queen Mother's eightieth birthday. It was to have been a grand evening, and Prince Charles was relaxed and happy, knowing that it was a very special occasion for his beloved grandmother. Practically all the members of the Royal Family were present, and 250 other guests besides. Throughout the evening Prince Charles circulated among them, chatting and joking. There is nothing unusual in that, for the Prince is very much in demand on such occasions and he is expected, as are other Royals, to try to talk to as many people as possible. An important guest is likely to feel very ruffled if he is left out. But, according to several guests who were present, he failed to return to Anna's side once during the whole evening. She felt she was being ignored, and at midnight headstrong Anna decided enough was enough. Her Scots blood 'up', she stormed over to the Prince and told him in a loud voice: 'Don't ever ignore me like that again. I've never been treated so badly in my life.'

Charles began to splutter an answer, but Anna delivered a final: 'No one treats me like that – not even you,' and turned on her heel and strode away. The outburst left Charles stunned and speechless . . . and Anna without a hope of becoming Britain's next Queen. A guest who saw it happen told me: 'It was just like a scene out of Cinderella – rushing out of the ball at midnight like that. Charles was quite upset because he was apparently very fond of her.'  .

The two never met again and it was not long before Anna married Lord Hesketh's younger brother, Johnny Hesketh. Anna was probably more at fault than Charles in the bust-up but her dramatic departure from the Prince's life highlights the fact that he can often appear to be over-casual in the way he treats women.

Even Lady Diana will be expected to walk a few paces behind him, before – and after – their marriage. It will take a considerate man to compensate for this by being as attentive as possible in other ways.

The three girls who were important in Prince Charles' life were: *Princess Marie-Astrid* of Luxembourg, *Davina Sheffield* and, above all, *Lady Jane Wellesley*. It would be difficult to think of three girls with such different qualities, looks and background but all of them could have been – might have been – a bride for the Prince of Wales.

The curious affair of Princess Marie-Astrid has been referred to earlier. Buckingham Palace has consistently denied any possibility of a royal marriage, but many unanswered questions remain.

'Asty', as she is known to her family and friends, is the blonde, blue-eyed daughter of Grand Duke Jean, whose friendship with the Queen goes back many years. A truly regal beauty, she is a trained nurse and perfectly suited, in terms of rank, title and pedigree, to share the British throne. Her name first began to be linked with the Prince's after the Queen made a state visit to Luxembourg in 1976. It was at a time when Charles was about to leave the Navy, and the Queen was desperately trying to help him find a bride. The Queen met 'Asty' and found her a 'delightful' girl. The problem was that the Princess – like Caroline of Monaco and Lucia Santa Cruz – was a Catholic and, under the Act of Settlement of 1701, no Catholic can become Britain's Queen. There have been several occasions when the Queen has considered pressing for the Act to be repealed; it has no purpose in the present age and the Queen felt that it was an unnecessary stumbling block. The Act got in the way when Prince Michael of Kent wanted to marry the Austrian-born Baroness Marie-Christine von Reibnitz, whose previous marriage had been annulled. The marriage was allowed to go ahead, but Prince Michael had to renounce his right of succession to the throne – he was then sixteenth in line.

There are conflicting accounts of whether or not Charles ever seriously considered Marie-Astrid, but in 1978 he delivered a curious speech about the 'needless distress' caused by doctrinal dispute among the churches. He spoke as Prince Michael's marriage was about to take place and his words may have been no more than an expression of sympathy for the Prince's plight. But some believe that Charles was thinking of his own position and was 'testing-out' public opinion. Marie-Astrid stayed in London for several months during 1977 to perfect her English and rumours persisted that she and Charles were destined for each other.

One secret never before revealed is that at one stage, the Freemasonry movement in Britain was full of talk that the Grand Duke was to be invested as a member of the same London lodge to which some member of the Royal Family belong. Freemasonry is anathema to many Catholics – for many years it was forbidden to them – and the theory was that, by joining the secret society, the Duke would be turning away from Catholicism and towards the Church of England. The way would then be paved for an Act of Parliament to repeal the Act, Marie-Astrid to change her religion and become Charles' bride.

The events never took place and, on 9 July 1980, Buckingham Palace ended speculation for ever with its second statement about the European princess: 'There are no plans whatsoever for a marriage between the Prince of Wales and Princess Marie-Astrid of Luxembourg – and there never have been.' Now that Charles has found a Protestant bride, his problems, on that score at least, are solved. But the Act of Settlement remains an antiquated legal obstacle which may yet unseat future royal romances, perhaps of Prince Charles' own children. And many aspects of the 'Marie-Astrid Affair' are a mystery which will probably never be solved.

But the last word goes to a close friend of the Prince, who told me that Charles did seriously view the prospect of marriage to Marie-Astrid, 'but after meeting her, he told me he thought she was very pretty – but a bit insipid'. By such judgements do royal marriages fall.

*Davina Sheffield* was a filly of a different colour, if she will forgive the expression. Tall (5 ft 11 in.), blonde – what else? – and decidedly attractive, Davina, the daughter of an Army major, stole the Prince's heart in the summer of 1976. They met at a dinner party given by Lady Jane Wellesley at her home in Fulham, and began to meet privately within days. After some weeks, the Prince invited Davina to spend August Bank Holiday weekend at Balmoral. Davina accepted the invitation and met the Royal Family much to the annoyance of Lady Jane, according to Chelsea gossip at the time. Davina, then twenty-five, and an ex-dèb, met the Prince again at various country homes of royal friends and at a wedding in Derbyshire. As the rumours flew, Davina played the 'no comment' game according to the book. Flashing a Queen-sized smile, she told reporters: 'It's really a very private matter. Possibly some people might think that it is something the public ought to know about. But I'm not making any comment, nor will I make any observations on what newspapers are saying.'

Davina was speaking at the time in the doorway of her £30,000 terraced home in Fulham, which she shared with her sister Laura. She did not know it, but sadly her days as number one companion to Prince Charles were already over. Certainly the Prince had been smitten with her. Then approaching his last few weeks in the Navy, a photograph of Davina, striding through sea spray wearing a big smile and a tiny bikini, took pride of place near the Prince's bunk in his cabin aboard the minesweeper HMS *Bronington*. He told shipmates she was a 'stunner'.

History – and a thousand newspaper cuttings – have recorded that the romance ended towards the end of 1976 over two incidents, one involving a nude Davina, and the other a previous boy-friend. In fact, Davina had said goodbye to St Paul's Cathedral, the Archbishop of Canterbury and all that much earlier – at their first Balmoral weekend. Davina was among a total of fourteen staying at the Royal Family's Scottish castle that memorable August, and Prince Charles was eager to show off the estate to her. But on the Saturday, the day of a shoot, he explained that the ladies remained at the castle while the men stalked the moors. Traditionally, he pointed out, the ladies joined the gentlemen by Range Rover at lunchtime to share a picnic. But soldier's daughter Davina was having none of it.

'I want to come with you,' she declared. Charles patiently explained again that the shoot involved long hours of walking over the moors. Davina eventually had her way, and Charles – not used to being crossed in such matters – deliberately stalked for miles and miles through the tangled gorse, Davina stumbling along behind as best she could. The Prince is a fit man and Davina was no match for him. That evening Davina failed to show for dinner. She was so exhausted that she remained in her bedroom. The Queen was put out. Quite apart from anything else, Davina's absence meant that thirteen were sitting down to dinner – and the Queen will never dine among that superstitious number.

'Where is Davina?' she enquired, solicitously.

Prince Charles shrugged his shoulders and replied: 'She wanted to walk – so I *walked* her.'

The Queen glared at him icily and declared: 'I don't think that was very kind.'

A special table for two had to be laid – to break up the unlucky thirteen – and the following morning Davina left in silence. The couple met on a few more occasions but the romance was all over bar the recriminations. Charles had long ago decided that a wife of his would have to know her place, and regard a request from her husband as little short of a command. Davina was too wilful.

The official seal was placed on the break-up not long afterwards when the story of Davina's naked encounter in a men's changing room reached the newspapers. Davina had been surfing with Charles off a secluded Devonshire beach he had discovered while under training at the Dartmouth Royal Naval College. He remembered the intimate cove when he returned there on an official visit in the *Bronington*. The Prince waited on the beach while Davina used the changing rooms of the local surf lifesaving club at Bantham, near Kingsbridge. Davina chose the men's changing room by mistake, and was down to the altogether when in walked burly beach guard Ray Atkinson. Davina stayed 'mum' when she rejoined Charles, but the secret was altogether too much for the beach guard to keep. His sighting of the girl, tipped as the future Queen, totally starkers kept him in free rounds for weeks. He told reporters, his eyes still popping: 'It was a great sight, but very unexpected. I bowled in without knowing she was there. She didn't bat an eyelid.'

To cap the matter once and for all, power-boat racing-driver James Beard then spilled the beans about the love-nest he and Davina had shared in an eleventh-century cottage, near Winchester, for nigh on six months. James had been 'miffed' when Davina broke off their unofficial engagement to spend time with Charles. Said James generously: 'I think Prince Charles is a very impressive man and I am sure they will be very happy. I think she will make an extremely good Queen and a magnificent wife.'

His words meant, of course, that she would never be anything of the kind. The glamorous interlude ended, but the complimentary postscript comes from the Prince who would say to friends for many months afterwards: 'I'll never forget Davina . . .'

*Lady Jane Wellesley* could well apply for the job of

'deputy Queen'. Second only to Lady Diana, and the Queen herself, she knows Prince Charles better than anyone else. She ought to, for their friendship lasted for four years. Again like Diana she had been a friend from childhood – Jane was a regular guest at Sandringham, Buckingham Palace and other royal homes. The Queen encouraged the romance, for Jane's father, the eighth Duke of Wellington, ranks among her most revered friends. Lady Jane shared Charles' sense of humour and love of animals. Her pet dog Napoleon – so named to celebrate the victory of her ancestor the 'Iron Duke' at Waterloo – went missing for two days, and the Prince shared her joy when he turned up safely.

The couple shared carefree holidays together on the family's 30,000-acre estate near Granada, in Spain, and on one occasion Jane was observed playfully tugging the Prince's hair and throwing melons at him. Their romance went on for so long that the public took it for granted that they would eventually marry. Jane was fourth in line behind the Queen Mother at a royal film premiere in London in 1974 – a classic sign of royal approval.

'Idiotic,' said the Duke of Wellington, when asked to comment on engagement rumours. But when Lady Jane was invited to Sandringham for the New Year, a crowd of 10,000 – some driving from fifty miles away – turned up to watch her attending Sunday morning service with the Prince. The following August, rumours reached fever pitch and 300 reporters and photographers made a bee-line for Strathfield Saye, the Wellington family seat in Berkshire, where the Queen and Prince Philip were visiting the annual Game Fair of the County Landowners' Association. It was the perfect occasion, all were convinced, for the betrothal to be announced. The fair, not surprisingly, was a tremendous success – but the Pressmen left empty-handed. The romance dwindled away like an early spring rose and Charles has been berated ever since for 'dithering' and 'missing his chance'.

Self-appointed authorities on the Royal Family have claimed that Prince Charles proposed and that Jane turned him down, or that Jane told him – without being asked – that she did not crave the life of a Queen. Neither theory is correct. Prince Charles was still serving in the Navy at the time, and was not mentally attuned to settling down. Moreover she had a quality of out-spokenness which occasionally ruffled the Prince of Wales' feathers. Jane, with more of the old 'Iron Duke' in her than most people realized, was very much a product of twentieth-century female emancipation. She joined the BBC as a researcher and was a vociferous 'father of the chapel' (chairman of her office union branch) of the National Union of Journalists. Over intimate dinner parties with the Prince in his quarters at Buckingham Palace, she would frequently amaze him with some of her more liberal views. Charles, an unashamed 'square', remarked afterwards: 'My word, some of her views are very left-wing.'

Jane, beautiful though she is, did not fit into the mould carefully prepared for the future Queen. Charles lost a potential wife, but gained a friend for life, and left his heart free for the girl who would one day capture it.

'Marriage,' said Prince Charles, 'is rather more than just falling madly in love with someone and having a love affair for the rest of your life. It is basically a very strong friendship. Creating a secure family unit in which to bring up children and give them a happy secure upbringing – that's what marriage is all about.'

# Chapter Seven

### 'You Mustn't Rush Me'

A JUMBLED mixture of thoughts must have been going through Prince Charles' mind as he stepped aboard a special RAF VC-10 at Heathrow Airport on 23 November at the beginning of what was to be the most gruelling, and perhaps decisive, tour of his life.

He was still angry about the royal train business, and sorry that Lady Diana had had to take the brunt of it alone. He was also a lonely man, for he was to have been accompanied on the tour by Lord Mountbatten who, as the last Viceroy of India, would have been not only excellent company but the perfect guide. The thirteen-day visit had originally been scheduled for the previous year, but India had been through a period of political instability at the time, and it was felt that it would be unwise for a member of the Royal Family to be seen to be involved. Buckingham Palace advisers feared that the Prince might be used by one side or the other for political kudos. By the time the tour was rescheduled Lord Mountbatten was dead and Prince Charles was left to face the punishing schedule by himself. He was accompanied by his personal staff, of course, including his Private Secretary, Edward Adeane; Press Officer, Warwick Hutchins; Equerry, Major John Winter; Group Captain Anthony Mumford of the Queen's Flight; his Scotland Yard bodyguards; Chief Inspector John MacLean; Sgt Jim McMaster; and his Valet, Ken Stronach.

Naturally, they were all loyal to their master, but they were not the sort of men with whom the Prince could discuss his very personal thoughts.

Mr Adeane had only been with the Prince since May 1979 – some eighteen months – and Mr Hutchins, a friendly New Zealander, had been appointed just a few months earlier and it was his first experience of a royal tour.

The private thoughts passing through the Prince's mind were of the nature only normally discussed with members of his own family; and who would have been better than 'Uncle Dickie' to help the Prince crystallize his decisions about the future. The long flight, away from the pressures of London, would have been the perfect opportunity. Now Charles had to keep his thoughts to himself. The Prince also had to concentrate his mind on the task ahead. Royal tours are more than just a flag-waving exercise. The Royal Family act as ambassadors for Britain, cementing trade as well as political relations, and India's teeming millions are a vast market. But the Prince was also to find that India, with its sacred temples and ancient monuments to pagan gods, has a strange effect on visitors by very often inspiring a major re-valuation of previously held views about human values and about life itself. Its poverty alone is a reminder of one's own blessings, for India is one place that could not be given a fresh coat of paint for a royal visit, and much of what the Prince saw came as a cultural shock.

The tour was also the first occasion that the Prince spoke openly about Lady Diana Spencer.

The visit began inauspiciously enough with practically empty streets in New Delhi, a city with a population of two million. The usual, enthusiastic bunting-clad welcome experienced by members of the Royal Family all over the world was replaced by small groups of people gazing with faint interest. Some thought it was the arrival of the South Korean President – others didn't care. Schoolchildren were not even given the day off. And the Prince arrived to the background of a fierce anti-British campaign in the Indian Press.

Political militants threatened demonstrations against Prince Charles because of the alleged 'inhuman treatment' of Asian immigrants in Britain. The *Sunday Standard*, one of India's most highly respected newspapers, called the tour 'a waste of time and money', and an editorial demanded to know: 'Why does Mrs Gandhi invite a person whose grandfather was thrown out of India by her own father?' (A

*Lady Diana at the nursery.* SUN

*The many faces of Lady Diana.* SUN

*The engagement is official.* ROTA

*Lady Diana leaves her flat the day after the engagement.* SUN

*Their first public sighting together after the engagement. The Prince and Lady Diana entering Lord Cholmondeley's private chapel in Cheshire.* SUN

*The author talks to Lady Diana. 'You know I can't talk about my feelings for him.'* SUN

*Lady Diana with her bodyguard, Chief Inspector Paul Officer, 'the man who saved Prince Charles's life.'* SUN

*Their first public appearance after the engagement. Lady Diana wearing 'that dress'.* SUN

reference to the fact that George VI was monarch at the time Nehru led India to independence.)

In fact there were only about thirty demonstrators on the drive to Rashtrapati Bhayan – the former Vice-regal lodge where Prince Charles stayed. The next day, however, was a different matter. A shouting, chanting mob of several hundred student demonstrators were waiting for Prince Charles when he arrived at Delhi University on one of his very first official engagements. Very different from the welcome extended to his great-uncle the previous Prince of Wales – an Emperor-of-India-to-be. 'WHITE FASCIST PIG,' their painted banners read, and 'CHARLES GO HOME.' The tension, as the mob jostled around him, got through to Charles and he lost his cool when a demonstrator repeatedly tried to push through to him with a petition, only to be bodily hurled back by baton-waving Indian policemen.

'Oh, come on then. Give me the bloody thing,' he snapped and the petition was handed over the heads of the crowd. It contained a protest against virginity tests on Asian women by immigration officers at Heathrow Airport, and Charles promised to read it later.

His outburst had the immediate effect of calming the situation, and a few minutes later he had cheered up sufficiently to joke about it. He told students in a packed lecture hall: 'I am Chancellor of the University of Wales back in Britain and, every time I visit one of the colleges, there is a demo. This is home away from home for me.'

By the time he left the university, Charles had won over the majority of the students. As he was passed a flower by a pretty Indian girl and thanked her, a boy at the back of the crowd called out: 'Why is it you always speak to the girls?'

Back came the answer, quick as a flash: 'Because they're always in front.'

The crowd's cheers outweighed the boos as his car pulled away.

The Indian newspapers, in the meantime, had received reports of the Lady Diana romance back in Britain, and came up with ideas of their own. 'Why doesn't he marry an Indian Princess?' suggested one. To those of us from Fleet Street, who were accompanying the Prince on his tour, it seemed that he had enough problems on his plate without considering *that* suggestion.

It was on the same day, during the open-air reception at the British High Commission in Delhi, that Charles ventured to speak about Lady Diana. It came after a hilarious incident, involving myself and colleague Arthur Edwards, which gave the party a lighthearted send-off.

The coverage of overseas tours had provided Fleet Street writers not only with fascinating glimpses of what the Royals are really like, but unforgettable experiences in exotic cities around the world. What happened in Delhi ranks among the most memorable.

Arthur had injured his back during the Delhi University riot, when he was pushed down a bank by the crowd. He was in considerable pain when we arrived back at our hotel with only a few minutes to change from slacks and shirts into formal suits before we were due to meet Prince Charles at the reception. We were already five minutes late when we met at the front door of the hotel and, as luck would have it, there wasn't a taxi in sight. The High Commission was less than a quarter of a mile away, but Arthur's injury meant that walking was out of the question. We waited a full ten minutes but no taxi appeared. Then I spotted the answer to our dilemma: 'parked' in a bay reserved for hotel guests' cars was an elephant. The animal was brought to the hotel most days to provide rides for tourists, but today was a quiet day and there he was, driver perched on his head, complete with 'howdah' for carrying passengers and decorated with coloured chalks and beads.

'Let's take the elephant,' I suggested, and Arthur – after a moment's pause – observed: 'Well, if we are going to meet the Prince of Wales, we might as well go in style.' A specially constructed set of wooden steps, ten-feet high, were placed beside the animal, and after climbing them we clambered into the 'howdah'. The days of the Raj seemed to have returned, as I ordered: 'Take us to the British High Commission, driver.'

As we set off through the dusty streets of Delhi, we must have looked an incongruous sight in the blazing sunshine, dressed in carefully pressed suits sitting atop a gaily painted elephant. The rocking motion against the unpadded seats did little for Arthur's back, and he groaned for most of the journey. But worse was to come. When we arrived at the High Commission there were no wooden steps, no ladder – no means of getting down. And from the top of a fully grown elephant, it's a surprisingly long drop.

'Jump,' suggested the Indian boy from the safety of his perch.

'Certainly not,' I replied. 'Make the elephant kneel down.' The animal obliged, accompanied by louder groaning noises beside me. There was still seven feet to go as I looked over the edge. A descent route was clearly needed.

'Put your right foot on the elephant's head,' I told Arthur. 'Then get hold of the right ear, and slide down.' The first part of the manoeuvre went perfectly, but Arthur missed his grip on the elephant's ear and fell sprawling in the roadway – on his back. I decided another route should be investigated and, climbing past the driver, shinned down the elephant's trunk. I had just arrived safely at ground level, coloured chalk smeared down the front of my suit, when Prince Charles arrived and climbed out of his car.

'What on earth are you two doing?' he asked with a laugh.

Arthur groaned his reply: 'Get someone to carry me in, give me a gin and tonic, and I'll tell you.'

The Prince enjoyed the joke and reminded us to be sure to claim for the elephant ride on our expenses. A few minutes later in the High Commission garden, a relaxed and good-humoured Prince sipped a glass of tonic water and responded to gentle probing about Lady Diana.

The writers present were desperately hoping he would say something definite about an engagement. A nod or a wink would have given us an instant front-page splash. But Charles, though clearly pleased to talk about Lady Diana, was careful to say nothing about the future. He seemed clearly undecided. After saying that – unlike other men – he could not live with a girl before marrying her, he said: 'You know, you mustn't rush me.'

The Prince, who was addressing a group of about five of us, went on: 'What you don't understand is that because a girl stays in the same house overnight, well, it isn't a case of "here we go, hooray and whoopee". It simply cannot be like that. In my position I have to live a rather old-fashioned life. And so do those in my circle.'

Paul Callan, the *Daily Mirror* columnist, remarked how well Lady Diana had coped under the pressure.

'That's kind of you to say so,' he replied. 'I must say I think she has been magnificent.' The admiration in his voice was unmistakable. Then, turning to me, Charles himself raised the question of the age-gap and why I had predicted in the *Sun* that Lady Diana was the one he would marry. 'Have you picked her out just because of her age?' he asked.

'Not at all, sir,' I replied. 'I picked her out because I think I could be forgiven for thinking that she is rather special in your life.' The Prince smiled but did not reply.

Then he caught me unaware with an embarrassing question. 'Is it right that you telephoned Nicky Soames, to ask when I was getting married?'

In fact I had phoned Mr Soames, the Prince's former equerry and son of Lord Soames, a few days earlier, in the hope that he might give me a pointer. I thought my call had been confidential, and I covered my embarrassment by exclaiming: 'Now look what you've done. Given away my best contact in front of the opposition.' (I should say, in fairness, that Mr Soames was not a true 'contact' nor did he give me any guidance.)

The Prince laughingly accepted my reply, and my difficult moment passed. Then he returned to the subject of Lady Diana and said enigmatically: 'You will all know in due course, but remember what I said, "Don't rush me".'

As we walked away across the lawns in the falling Delhi dusk, I was left with the unmistakable impression that here was a man on the very knife-edge of making a momentous decision.

But many more weeks were to pass before the world knew the outcome. As the tour proceeded and the royal party crisscrossed the vast sub-continent, Charles – now in his stride – turned the visit, from its ominously slow start, into a resounding success. He was garlanded and cheered wherever he went, and he responded by amusing his hosts with down-to-earth humour. In Jaipur, where he stayed with one of India's last remaining princely families, he addressed an immense gathering of 25,000 farmers under the biggest canopy tent any of us had ever seen, and delighted them with a closing message in their local dialect, Gujarati. Roughly translated, the words meant: 'May the udders of your buffaloes always be full of milk'.

All good copy, but by now the photographers were becoming desperate for pictures. For it had been the policy from the outset that the Prince would be shown the modern India of model farms and machine-tool factories, not the India of elephants and tiger shoots experienced by his great-uncle David – later Edward VIII – nearly sixty years earlier. It is a fact of life in the media world that pictures of machine-tool factories do not get into popular newspapers (and, for that matter, not very often into so-called 'heavy' newspapers), while pictures of Prince Charles sitting on an elephant do. The day was saved, photographically speaking, on reaching Bombay, when a beautiful sixteen-year-old Indian actress gave Charles a lingering kiss during his visit to a film studio.

It made a front-page picture – not without a little prior help from the enterprising photographers, who had assured the actress, Padmini Kolhapure, that it was customary in England to greet princes with a kiss, and that he might be offended if he didn't get one. It helped matters, too, when Padmini turned out to be playing the part of a budding prostitute in the film she was making, and that she was known to her fans throughout India as their equivalent of the 'Oomph Girl'.

The Prince, who was in fine humour, readily agreed when she asked if she could kiss him. 'Why not?' he said, 'Everyone else does.'

The kiss gave the Prince the excuse to ask if she kissed in the film and whether she ever got involved in 'bedroom scenes'.

'Never,' she said.

'Well, that must make life easier,' he grinned. Lady Diana would have blushed to the roots of her hair had she been there.

As the tour wore on, there were times when it seemed to some of us that the Prince's thoughts were elsewhere. He received almost daily reports from London, despite the difficulties of the telephone, and the news was mixed.

The royal train row was still rumbling on, and Lady Diana was the centre of another disputed story – this time over an interview 'that never was'. She had been quoted at length in the London evening paper, apparently giving her views on marriage.

The quotes included the following: 'I'd like to marry soon. What woman doesn't want to marry eventually?' Next year? 'Why not? I don't think nineteen is too young – it depends on the person.' She was said to have expressed the view that age didn't matter in marriage, adding that she loved children. And when asked if Prince Charles had proposed to her, Lady Diana was reported to have laughed and said: 'I can't say "yes" or "no" to that. I can't confirm or deny it.'

In another, separate interview about Charles, Lady Diana was quoted as saying: 'I wanted to see him this weekend – before he went to India. But we decided it was better not to get together because of all the fuss and bother it would have caused.'

On the same day as the first interview was alleged to have been given, Lady Diana went on record to deny it. Reading the report on the Press Association news tape, she said: 'It's simply not true. I didn't say any of this. I never said anything about marriage.' She added: 'I'm terribly worried about it. It's very upsetting.'

The other news from London was that, according to rumour, the Prime Minister of Australia had been given an early warning about the wedding, and *Debrett's Peerage*, the 'bible' of the aristocracy, was ready to roll with *Debrett's Book of the Royal Wedding*, after being given a tip by the Palace. Managing director Harold Brook-Baker was quoted as saying: 'Lady Diana is considered a serious candidate by the Royal Family. She is a very attractive person, and she has a very impressive ancestry,' adding wistfully, 'Mind you, Princess Marie-Astrid had an unbelievably impressive ancestry.'

Finally, Lady Diana's mother wrote to *The Times* complaining of the lies told about her daughter:

> In recent weeks many articles have been labelled 'exclusive quotes' when the plain truth is that my daughter has not spoken the words attributed to her. Fanciful speculation, if it is in good taste, is one thing, but this can be embarrassing.
>
> Lies are quite another matter, and by their very nature hurtful and inexcusable.

If any of the reports upset Prince Charles, he showed no sign of it.


The tour swept on – staggered on for some, after attacks of 'Delhi Belly', as the entourage christened it, began to take its toll. Press Officer Hutchins was among the victims. Fortunately, as is the case with all royal tours, Prince Charles was constantly attended by a doctor. Dr Jim Campbell, a beaming Scotsman seconded from the British High Commission, was never more than a few feet from the Prince's side. But as the Prince himself never seemed to get ill, the good doctor became almost permanently attached to the Press corps. At 'sick parade' each morning, he would enquire of the ailment with a cheerful 'up, or down?' When the answer was 'down', as invariably it was, he prescribed a particularly powerful drug. When one photographer asked what effect the drug had, he replied: 'It's rather like having half a ton of premixed concrete tipped down you.'

Thus the travelling show was kept on the road.

It was not long before the subject of love and marriage arose again. On reaching Agra, the Prince paid a memorable visit to the Taj Mahal, the incredibly beautiful marble edifice which ranks as one of the wonders of the world. Earl Mountbatten used to tell Charles that the proper way to see the Taj Mahal was by moonlight, but the Prince chose the next best time, just as the sun was going down. After the Prince had toured the monument, Independent Television reporter Kate Adey seized the opportunity to score over her female BBC rival and leapt in for the first words from the Prince, spoken to camera, since the tour began.

'What did you think of the Taj Mahal, sir?' she asked, the camera rolling.

The question had to be asked even though it was practically impossible to answer off the cuff. What do you say about a tomb built more than three centuries ago by a grief-stricken emperor as a tribute of love to a wife who bore him fourteen children and died in childbirth – and which took an army of 20,000 craftsmen twenty-two years to complete? Avoiding all the clichés, the Prince paused a second or two and replied: 'It was a marvellous idea, to build something so wonderful . . . to someone one loved so very much.'

There is a legend about the Taj that every man who visits it alone will one day return with his wife. The next question was an obvious one, but – such was the delicate state of relations between Buckingham Palace and the Press at that moment – none of us dared ask it. But an Indian reporter, either braver than the rest of us – or simply ignorant of the row back in London – chipped in: 'Will you come back again?'

When he received the answer: 'Yes I'd like to,' he immediately replied.

'And will you bring your wife?'

'He'll never answer that one,' murmured Ann Morrow of

the *Daily Telegraph*. The Prince's notoriously fast return of service failed him for just a second of two, then his face broke into a huge grin as he said: 'I might take up the Muslim religion and have lots of wives. That would be much more fun.'

Once more, Prince Charles won through with his humour. And the Indian reporters loved him even more when he parried the next question with rapier speed.

'Sir,' he was asked, 'Were you touched by the Taj Mahal?'

Quick-as-a-flash came the reply: 'Well, I did bang my head against the ceiling at one point.'

The humour aside, it will be fascinating to see whether one day Prince Charles returns to the monument of love with Lady Diana as his wife and princess.

Pressmen, who had hoped for another clue from the Prince about his engagement before the return to Britain, began to grow desperate as the tour entered its final days. But Prince Charles was by now unapproachable on the subject, and his aides were pressed daily for any snippets they might have picked up from him about the future. Edward Adeane and Warwick Hutchins replied to every question, however artfully put, with polite but negative replies. Looking back, it seems certain that they could not have helped, even had they wished to. For they, like everyone else, simply did not know.

Two more experiences awaited Prince Charles before the tour ended, and, though starkly in contrast with one another, each was in its own way revealing. En route to the first, the photographers finally got the picture they wanted – Prince Charles with an elephant. He was not astride it as they had hoped, but came across it 'by chance' when it blocked the road and brought his motorcade to a halt – another inspired example of Fleet Street giving fate a helping hand. The Prince, recognizing the 'set-up', nevertheless obliged and walked across to the elephant. But when it attempted to place a garland of flowers round his neck with its trunk, the elephant misjudged the manoeuvre and came close to clouting Charles on the head.

'That was a close call,' said the Prince as he ducked.

'More of a trunk call, I would have thought,' remarked a voice in the Press corps.

Another front-page picture. The Prince moved on to the 'Temple of Love' at Konarak where an amazing sight was stretched before him. The ancient Sun Temple of the Hindus is a major attraction for tourists, not so much for its undoubted archaeological interest but for the thousands of statues, carved from stone, which adorn it. For they show naked men and women in every conceivable – and inconceivable – position of love-making. The sheer size of the temple is impossible to convey. As the Prince was shown around the ruins – a sort of guided tour of the *Kama Sutra* in stone – he gazed unbelievingly at the statues and, eyeing the microphones around him, kept his mouth firmly closed. The Indian guide pointed to a carving of a bird perched on a naked woman's arm and said, enthusiastically, 'Look, he's kissing her breast!'

Even then the Prince managed to move his lips without actually saying anything. Finally the guide tried to drag him by the arm to the best vantage point for viewing a massive carving more than ten feet high of a naked couple engaged in a particular sexual act, popularly known as '*soixante neuf*'.

'It's quite all right,' said the Prince politely. 'I can see quite well from here, thank you.'

'But you must,' insisted the guide. 'It's the main attraction for everyone who comes to the temple.'

Mr Adeane gently removed the guide's hand from the royal arm and remarked drily: 'That rather depends on who you are, doesn't it?'

Prince Charles chuckled with the rest of us and walked on. Later he told me: 'I was dying to point at some of the statues and say "Look at that one, and that one" but I knew the picture would go straight into the *Sun*.'

He was perfectly correct, of course.

The tour of India ended in Calcutta, a city where civilization appears to the European to have totally broken down, and where abject poverty is an accepted way of life.

Hundreds of thousands live under blankets and cardboard shelters on the pavements, and the dead are picked up from the street at dawn each day. Charles was shocked – and embarrassed too by the Rolls-Royce carrying him on a tour of the city. He suggested changing to another car on the grounds that he couldn't see the people properly, and travelled for the rest of the day in a far less ostentatious Mercedes.

He was finally moved to tears when he visited the orphanage run by Nobel Peace Prize winner Mother Teresa, the seventy-year-old nun who shares the poverty of the people she serves. Tears welled up in his eyes when he saw the matchstick-thin children who had been rescued from the gutters, and a three-day-old baby girl found abandoned in a dustbin.

'What will happen to her – will she be adopted?' he asked.

Mother Teresa told him that the little girl *would* be adopted. Others were not so lucky. The Prince seemed to be sharing the thoughts of all of us as he looked with compassion at the little bundle.

'Wouldn't you like to take her home?' he asked a reporter, as though considering the same proposition for himself. It was out of the question, of course, but he might have been contemplating, too, the life that child will grow to live compared with his own children. Before he left the orphanage, Prince Charles joined Mother Teresa in prayer in the Chapel of the Immaculate Heart of Mary. The Prince and the pauper knelt side by side and prayed for the poor and the sick in the world's most overcrowded city.

For a man who will be king, with unimaginable riches, it was a humbling experience and I believe that Prince Charles left India a wiser and more experienced man. His eyes could never be closed again to the privilege of his position compared with countless millions. Afterwards he said, simply: 'It was very moving, and it made me realize that in our country we have no poverty compared with what these people suffer.'

I also believe that India helped Charles unclutter his mind

about what he wanted to do with the rest of his life.

The slog of the Indian tour was followed by seven days of comparative relaxation in Nepal, the world's last surviving Hindu monarchy. Outdoor lover that he is, he trekked for three days in the foothills of the Himalayas, with a retinue of ninety porters, twenty-one Sherpas, and a support party of eleven, all to ensure he could be alone.

He returned with a delightfully scruffy three-day-old growth of beard, and looking exhilarated. Then, after telling a joke about the legendary Yeti that would have made Lady Diana's hair curl, he set off for home in the brightest mood we had seen for many months.

But he was returning to the pressures of London, and more questions about his engagement. As the VC-10 headed for Heathrow, his mood swiftly faded.

# Chapter Eight

## The Storm Before the Calm

A CLEAN-SHAVEN Prince Charles stepped down from the plane to find a jostling throng of photographers waiting to meet him. Prince Charles and Lady Diana were still front-page news, and the whole country was waiting expectantly.

Photographers the world over have developed a technique of walking backwards, snapping as they go, when they are covering a moving subject. And as the Prince walked rapidly across the tarmac, one of them knocked over a large metal container. The Prince winced as it hit the ground with a mighty crash.

He commanded: 'Now pick it up. Anyone would think there was a war going on.' He strode to his waiting car, took the wheel and pulled away so fast the engine almost stalled.

There followed one of the unhappiest interludes of modern times in the delicately balanced relationship between the Queen and the Press. The strain over whether or not the wedding was ever going to take place was without doubt at the root of it. For we know now that by Christmas and the New Year, Prince Charles still had not proposed. And at one stage, the Queen said to a member of her household: 'Even I don't know what's going on.'

The phrase 'Press harassment' began to crop up with unhealthy frequency but there are many who believe the fault lay on both sides – if faults there were. Prince Charles, when he was away from the rest of the Royal Family, coped very well. But when he rejoined them, the Press followed and the Queen found herself under siege. Royal tempers became frayed and for a while it seemed like open war.

After the Prince returned from India he and Lady Diana did not see each other for several weeks – or, at least, if they did it was, understandably, with total secrecy. Lady Diana, who had told friends she had missed the Prince and was 'looking forward to seeing him again', developed 'flu and they spent Christmas apart.

'I feel quite dreadful,' she said, though she was comforted by the Prince's regular telephone calls.

He joined the Royal Family at Sandringham, where the photographers were beginning to encamp, for the traditional New Year's holiday. The Royal Family have become accustomed, over the years, to Fleet Street's interest in the Sandringham New Year break and have, in the past, happily co-operated. But the engagement rumours attracted a bigger Press contingent than usual, and the Queen was in no mood for photographs. Cameramen who tried to photograph Princess Anne's son riding his Shetland pony finally made her snap. Fearing they might upset the toddler, she told them: 'I wish you would go away.'

A journalist who watched from the roadway as members of the Royal Family walked across the fields, shooting pheasants, had her car peppered with shot, and there were heated arguments with local police officers about the law which determines how far from a roadway a shotgun may be discharged. A photographer also standing in the roadway had the unnerving experience of a shotgun being fired over his head.

Back in London, the Buckingham Palace Press office weighed in with the comment that the Queen was finding the intrusion 'intolerable'. 'She is more than a little angry,' said a spokesman. The photographers didn't have to be told that – they were caught between the Queen's wrath, and the instructions from the picture desks to keep watching for Lady Diana. It is difficult, even now, to see what else they could have done – except keep a discreet distance, which I for one can vouch they did.

Newspapers like *The Times* and *Telegraph*, who were by now telephoning the Palace Press office with queries about 'Press harassment', were told that the Queen had specifically asked the Press to stay away from Sandringham. No newspaper office ever received any such request. And the 'quality' newspapers, fearing they might be missing something, sent their own staffmen to Sandringham – and were joined by television teams. They were able to justify their presence under the guise of covering the 'harassment' as a news story, but inside Sandringham a member of the Royal Family said: 'Make no mistake, they are here to watch us.'

Evidently, the Royals were not fooled. Four days into the New Year, Prince Charles reflected the Queen's displeasure when he walked across to a group of us, patiently waiting outside in the cold at Sandringham, with a message: 'I would like to take this opportunity,' he said, 'of wishing you all a Happy New Year, and your editors a particularly nasty one.'

Arthur Edwards replied: 'Well, I don't wish you anything nasty, Sir – Happy New Year.'

The reply caught the Prince by surprise and he said, 'That's very kind – thank you.'

The Prince was to admit later that, although he had made the remark after careful forethought, he regretted it afterwards. His dig at Fleet Street editors, combined with the Queen's outburst – the first on record in her reign – had the effect of producing a number of leader articles in daily newspapers criticizing the Queen. Things were getting badly out of hand, and the Press office did not help by continually adding to the back-biting. Now was the right moment to take up the suggestion of one Fleet Street editor to call all the editors to the Palace for an off-the-record friendly chat. The situation could have been defused overnight. But no such plan was put into action – for the simple reason that Prince Charles still had not proposed.

The *Sun*'s leader article of 5 January contained the reminder that the Royal Family needs the newspapers as much as the country needs the Royal Family and it delivered a slap on the wrist for the Queen's Press Secretary. It read:

> The Queen is said to be angry about the unusually large number of photographers outside the Royal estate at Sandringham.
>
> It is reported they are spoiling her Christmas holiday

which is due to last five weeks. The *Sun* – along with the rest of Fleet Street, no doubt – is sorry if she is upset. Nobody wants to ruin the Queen's well-earned holiday. But it must be pointed out that Press coverage on this scale need not have happened if the Palace had come clean about whether or not Lady Diana Spencer would be staying at Sandringham.

They could have said either 'No, Lady Diana will not be with the Royal Family' or 'Yes, she will be a guest, so let us have a single organised session with Press photographers.'

Under an arrangement like this, the Royal Family could have been left to get on with their holiday in peace. Instead there is an unpleasant atmosphere made worse by the occasional loss of cool from the Royal side of the fence.

For instance, reporters and photographers moving on *public* roads *do* have the right to expect that their vehicle will not be peppered by gunshot by shooting parties which include Prince Philip and Prince Charles. It is sad that the normally good relations between the Palace and the Press should be strained like this. There is, after all, tremendous respect for the Royal Family.

The Monarch is now held in a higher esteem than ever – thanks partly to the major reporting role played by the popular Press but the unfortunate – and we believe temporary – breakdown in good relations has hardly been helped by Mr Michael Shea, the Press Secretary (or should it be anti-Press Secretary) to the Queen.

His 'contribution' has been to leak to the posh papers the information that the Queen is being hounded and this he knows to be pure fiction. The claim by 'a Palace spokesman' (no doubt the same Mr Shea) that the Queen is now considered 'fair game' by Fleet Street even when on private holiday is misleading and mischievous. The Press is not there to persecute her. Its natural and legitimate goal is to photograph the lady who may be the next Queen of England.

112

Similar articles appeared in other newspapers.

On 8 January, Prince Charles took the heat out of the 'siege' by quitting Sandringham to travel to his Gloucestershire home – and Lady Diana joined him for their first get-together in weeks. They had a great deal to talk about, but even at this late stage – with the engagement only weeks away – Lady Diana was in the dark about her future, as I afterwards learned.

From Highgrove, Lady Diana accompanied Prince Charles to Lambourn to watch him exercise his horse Allibar. The Prince was in a bright mood as he cycled the short distance from the stables to the home of his trainer, Nick Gaselee.

'Good morning,' he said to Pressmen. 'You are all up early!' We were. It was 6.15 a.m.

As he raced by, he called to Arthur Edwards: 'I don't know how you manage to get the pictures in focus when I'm going so fast.'

'Well, slow down then,' shouted Arthur.

'I mustn't,' the Prince called over his shoulder. 'I'm trying to keep fit.'

A few days later, Lady Diana travelled to Sandringham for one of the most vital weekends of her life. Any other young girl would have called it 'going to meet my potential mother-in-law'. For Lady Diana it was the last 'test' of her suitability as a royal bride – the Queen's final approval. She was invited specifically as a guest of the Queen, rather than of Charles – the difference is crucial.

The Queen, Prince Philip, Charles and Lady Diana stayed at Wood Farm, a small, red brick building hidden behind trees on the Sandringham estate. While the two men went out shooting during the daytime, the Queen and Diana spent hours talking alone in the comfortably furnished lounge.

It was the best opportunity they would ever have of getting to know each other as people; and, for the Queen, of judging the character of her future daughter-in-law. They spent several more hours walking across the fields on the estate, and they laughed a lot together.

Once again elaborate arrangements were made for Lady Diana to arrive and depart unseen. And when the Queen bade her farewell, she told Lady Diana, 'I'm sorry we have to smuggle you in and out like this, but I'm afraid it is something you will have to get used to for the time being.'

*Prince Charles had made up his mind.* Officially, Lady Diana did not know, but Prince Charles had told his parents a few days earlier that Diana was his choice. There remained only behind-the-scenes arrangements before Prince Charles could make his move.

The following weekend, Charles and Diana were together at Sandringham again, and the Prince's undisguised happiness convinced even the most sceptical of Sandringham's staff that Charles had found a bride at last. A Royal aide told me at the time: 'With so much speculation in the air, the Queen would not have encouraged Lady Diana to visit Sandringham if it were thought that this was just another of Prince Charles' short-lived romances.'

That weekend, Charles and Diana teamed up with Princess Anne and Mark Phillips for a private shooting party and the basis of a close friendship was formed between Anne and Diana. 'If they are to become royal sisters-in-law, they have made a good start,' I was told.

Lady Diana was already becoming part of the family. When the weekend was over, Diana returned to London with a police escort, and the Prince, left to his own devices again, returned to the hunting field.

Then, at the height of the speculation, Prince Charles went off on his skiing holiday. For months there had been forecasts as to whether or not Lady Diana would accompany him – and right up to the last moment no firm decision was made. Prince Charles, who has come to love the annual break in Switzerland as his favourite holiday of the year, was dying to show Diana the beauty of the Alpine slopes, and share his relaxation. Diana was not so sure.

Photographers from publications throughout Europe were not sure either, but they went along just in case. They could not know that, with a day to go before the Prince was due to leave, Lady Diana decided that her presence would ruin the Prince's holiday and she reluctantly stayed behind.

On his first morning in Switzerland, Charles was in a decidedly bad mood when he emerged from his chalet to find the assembly of cameras outside. For five days, the Prince went out of his way to make photographs difficult. Once he had reached the top of a ski run, he would endeavour to disappear – at high speed – for the rest of the day. And when he *was* spotted, he obstinately refused to smile.

After five days of no worthy pictures – and Lady Diana still in London – the Continental photographers gave up and pulled out, leaving just four journalists, two each from the *Sun* and *Daily Mirror*, and freelance photographer Tim Graham, who is well known to the Royal Family. Only then did Charles relax. As his tan deepened in the bright sunshine of the mountains, so his spirits lifted.

Enjoying the freedom of his holiday as a bachelor, I believe Prince Charles cleared his mind of any remaining doubts he might have had. Every day, he found time to stop and have a friendly chat with the five of us. He was by now enjoying the secret he was keeping from us, and we spoke of everything bar Lady Diana. I made up my mind that I would make one last attempt for the exclusive we had been working for, and decided to ask the Prince point-blank whether he was going to marry Lady Diana. But before doing so, I turned for advice to two ladies: Patty Palmer-Tompkinson, who as usual was the Prince's hostess for the holiday – and Lady Diana herself.

Patty's answer, when I found her in a quiet moment, was straight and to the point: 'Please don't,' she said. 'He's so relaxed and laid-back – it would destroy his holiday.'

Then I telephoned Lady Diana as I had done so many times before. I heard the international operator's voice telling her: 'Lady Diana, I have a call from Klosters for you.'

When I announced who I was, she burst into a fit of giggles. 'Well, who did you think it was?' I asked. 'Who else could it be?' And Diana went into another giggling fit. When I told her what I intended to do, she was unsure.

'I really don't know what to say,' she said, and then added a revealing comment. 'You know, people keep asking me questions, but I'm the last person in the world who knows what's going on.'

The telephone conversation between Klosters and Old Brompton Road, London, continued for just over an hour. Lady Diana was fascinated by any news of the Prince, and I told her how he was enjoying his break. It was the last conversation I was to have with her before it became impossible, because of the engagement, ever to reach her again. Perhaps, one day, at a more formal occasion we may be able to speak together again. For those to whom Lady Diana went out of her way to be so friendly and courteous before her engagement, the days of 'Hello, Di' are over for ever.

I took Patty's advice and decided not to put the $64,000 question to the Prince. There seemed little hope, in any case, that he would give a reply.

The skiing holiday drew to an end, but not before the incident which I like to think of as 'the blonde who nearly ruined the engagement'. In previous years in Klosters, when the Prince had still been very much a bachelor, he had often been photographed with one beautiful girl or another.

On one occasion, Miss Switzerland skied straight into him 'by accident' and the Prince obliged by helping her up, even though he knew it was another set-up. But on this last holiday he made doubly sure not to be seen with anyone who could remotely be described as a pretty girl. It was amazing, therefore, when a beautiful blue-eyed blonde emerged from the chalet one evening, just after the Prince had gone in after a day's skiing.

I had been waiting outside with Arthur Edwards to check that the Prince had returned safely. (There were previous occasions when he had been injured skiing and it was part of our duties to ensure each day that the heir to the throne was unharmed.) When the blonde walked past me, I stopped her and politely asked who she was and why she had been at the chalet. It was perfectly innocent, of course. The girl, a Swiss, had been delivering a message. But a few moments later as we walked past the chalet, Prince Charles emerged on the low balcony, and called out: 'You aren't worried about that young lady, are you?'

I assured him that we weren't, and my collegue told him, with a laugh, that she had been 'checked out'.

The Prince smiled and looked relieved. Then he asked, 'How do you do that? Do you run them through a computer?'

I explained that in fact we always checked the girls in his life by simply talking to them. But, referring to the blonde, I added, 'I looked into her big blue eyes and couldn't think of a question!'

'Yes, she was rather pretty, I must say,' Charles commented, thoughtfully. But he was content that no story or picture was going back to London about 'Charles and the mystery blonde', and he happily retired for the night.

The following day, Prince Charles left the chalet to return home. After ten days of dressing in ski gear, he emerged once more as the Prince of Wales, in formal suit, tie and grey overcoat.

His friends, the Palmer-Tompkinsons, said goodbye and Patty, still dressed in a ski suit, curtsied incongruously in the snow outside. For over a week the two had shared the tiny chalet with Charles and his detective, living like a family. But now Patty was a commoner again, and Charles was a Prince. As he began to walk up the steep incline to his car, Prince Charles, who was wearing ordinary shoes, began to slip on the ice. His detective grabbed one arm, Charlie Palmer-Tompkinson the other, and they lifted and carried him the rest of the way.

As though in a last fling, a final goodbye to his carefree bachelor days, Charles broke into his favourite voice from *The Goon Show* and began to sing: '*They're coming to take me away, ho-ho, hee-hee, ha-ha.*'

He waved farewell as he set off in the British Ambassador's car for Zurich Airport, for London and the last act of the engagement drama.

# Chapter Nine

## 'Sir . . . I will'

PRINCE CHARLES' blue-painted sitting-room in his cramped quarters on the second floor of Buckingham Palace, overlooking the Mall, is his favourite room. It contains a veritable treasure trove of objects he has collected from all over the world, the personal mementoes which mean most to him. Some are priceless – others have no particular value except to the Prince himself. In the centre of the room is a suite of chairs and a sofa around a coffee table.

It was there that the Prince of Wales finally popped the question: 'Will you marry me?' It happened on Wednesday, 4 February, 1981, after Charles and Diana had shared a romantic candlelit dinner together. The Prince had returned, refreshed, only two days earlier from Switzerland, and he knew he did not have much time. For on the following Saturday, Lady Diana was due to leave England with her mother and stepfather for an away-from-it-all holiday in Australia. It had been planned in secret for some time and, though it meant another separation for the couple, it suited Prince Charles' purposes because, in true Royal tradition, he wanted Lady Diana to have a chance to think it over – 'time to think if it was all going to be too awful.' Of that very private moment between two people we know only what the couple revealed afterwards. Prince Charles wanted Diana to give her answer on her return. But Diana did not hesitate. She said 'Yes' straight away.

'I never had any doubts about it,' she explained.

It was an historic moment for both of them. The Prince's search was over, and he had chosen the girl he wanted by his side for the rest of his life. And for Diana, not so very long out of school, shy, and with no pretensions about her, a whole new world was about to open up. With her acceptance of the Prince's proposal came the awful realization that one day she would become Queen of the most prestigious and historic monarchy in the world.

As she reflected upon her reply, Lady Diana may even have reacted with the delightful giggle which has become her hallmark at moments of nervousness.

That moment of promised betrothal lifted a tremendous burden from both their shoulders. The tension and pressure which had surrounded them for months began to drift away. They had only to get through the next few weeks without letting the secret slip. For royal engagements cannot be announced at the drop of a hat. First all the members of the Royal Family had to be told; then the Archbishop of Canterbury, the Prime Minister and the heads of the Commonwealth. A thousand and one arrangements would have to be made for the engagement day itself. The administrative machinery of Buckingham Palace would have to be given time to move into first gear. Prince Charles was determined as ever that no one outside that enclave of those-who-must-be-told would hear even the slightest whisper of what was to happen, until he was ready. The Australian holiday would provide the ideal breathing space. While Lady Diana relaxed in the sunshine, the master plan could be put into operation.

The following weekend, the Prince's own staff helped Lady Diana slip unnoticed out of Heathrow with her mother and stepfather, Frances and Peter Shand Kydd. It was no mean feat, for Britain's premier airport is the permanent base of a whole team of Fleet Street photographers; it even has its own news agency. But they managed it. Lady Diana left her flat the night before the flight and stayed at a friend's house.

The following morning, the trio boarded Quantas flight QF2 and arrived in Sydney on the Sunday morning. From there they travelled to the Shand Kydds' sheep and cattle station, Good Hope Farm, near Yass, in New South Wales. Lady Diana's disappearance caused pandemonium in Fleet Street. Only someone who had been painstakingly, but discreetly, reporting upon the Prince of Wales' romantic life for several years could appreciate the near-panic which set in. Where was she? And what did her absence mean?

Within twenty-four hours I was able to establish for the *Sun* – along with only one other newspaper – that Lady Diana, was without doubt, in Australia. But that was as far as my information went, and to have pursued the mystery to the point of flying to Australia could not be justified when set against the cost. The problem was handed over to Australian journalists and, over the humming international telephone lines, they received a great deal of good natured ribbing over their failure to 'find the lady'.

Enquiries at Good Hope Farm provoked this sort of reply from Mrs Shand Kydd: 'Diana is not here and is not coming here. She is certainly on holiday but not in Australia. I know where she is, but of course I'm not saying where. Diana has gone somewhere sunny. We are here for six weeks and we do not expect to hear from any of our children except by mail until we return.'

As if the message needed underlining, Mr Shand Kydd added: 'Lady Diana is on a different continent.'

The search went on at an increasingly desultory pace until the 'Aussies' plainly gave up. On reflection, it was just as well that they failed to find her, for it meant that Lady Diana was able to enjoy the last few days of her freedom as a single girl in peace and tranquillity.

For ten days she relaxed in a private house on a beach in New South Wales, swimming, surfing and soaking up the sun. In between time, she told her mother of the marriage proposal, and of her acceptance and together they discussed her future. It was a brief respite, but one which Lady Diana thoroughly enjoyed. She was never to be so free again.

Lady Diana flew alone out of Australia before Pressmen there had categorically confirmed she had even arrived but, to be fair to my antipodean colleagues, she slipped through the net again at Heathrow. Special clearance had been arranged with customs and immigration, which helped considerably. It caused a security row among Heathrow staff at the time, but the short cut arranged by Buckingham Palace was forgivable. Lady Diana was hardly likely to have been smuggling anything. More importantly, the VIP treatment was the latest in the growing number of clues that something *was* afoot, and royal writers went on the alert. Lady Diana's mother had, of course, been misleading journalists all along. 'Misleading' is a gentle word for it.

'I lied through my teeth,' she admitted later. 'I have no regrets. I was determined to have what my daughter and I knew to be our last holiday together. I chose Australia because it's a country for which I have great affection. The people there were marvellous – they succeeded in concealing us for ten days.'

Lady Diana, for her own part, was embarrassed by the deception. Back at her flat, she said, 'My mother told everybody I wasn't in Australia to protect me. She wanted me to have a rest, to get away from people. Whatever I may feel, I know why she did it.' (Fleet Street made a mental note for the future that, contrary to popular belief, the aristocracy do sometimes tell fibs, and occasionally outrageous 'whoppers'.)

During Lady Diana's absence, Prince Charles had gone about his ordinary engagements and was anxious not to do anything out of pattern which might 'give the game away'.

The couple were eagerly looking forward to seeing each other again, and the royal writers were naturally wondering what was going on. Temporarily diverted by Prince Andrew's twenty-first birthday celebrations – or rather the lack of them – in Cornwall, where he is stationed at the Culdrose Royal Naval Air Station, we were soon alerted that Lady Diana was back in the country. Her reappearance in London did not go entirely unnoticed. She was spotted shopping for a new outfit in her favourite shop, Harrods. (Now that *was* interesting.)

The reunion came at Highgrove, where Lady Diana stayed the night – one of many during the last weeks of their courtship – before accompanying him on the Saturday morning (21 February) to the Lambourn, Berkshire, home of his trainer Nick Gaselee. Prince Charles, a keen amateur rider, had been in training to ride his eleven-year-old hunter Allibar in the Cavalry Hunter Chase the following day. Charles, who had twice been placed second in earlier outings, was keen to win a race though he advised me, after learning I had lost £5.00 on him last time out, 'Don't bet on me – I'm on a losing streak!'

Prince Charles had gone to Lambourn for his regular practise gallop. For the *Sun* team – having lost sight of Lady Diana for some weeks – it was gratifying literally to catch up with her on the M4 motorway as she sat in the front of the Prince's estate car, the Prince at the wheel, en route from Highgrove to Lambourn.

We were the only newspaper present as Prince Charles and Lady Diana arrived together, but none of us could know the tragedy which within minutes would strike the couple, and which perhaps brought them closer than they had ever been.

Prince Charles mounted up and set off for the nearby Downs, Lady Diana following in a Land Rover accompanied by two Scotland Yard officers. As the Prince rode out, Arthur Edwards took the last photograph of him astride Allibar, for moments later the horse was dead. At the end of the first gallop, Prince Charles had slowed to a canter and felt the horse tremor beneath him. He dismounted and the gelding keeled over before his eyes. He cradled the stricken horse's head in his arms, buy by the time the vet arrived it was all over. Lady Diana stood watching with tears streaming down her cheeks, and the Prince looked close to crying as he slowly walked back to her. The couple comforted each other as they returned to the trainer's home.

The Prince had become fond of Allibar, for which he paid £15,000 and is said to have spent long periods alone talking to the animal. Allibar's death, from a heart attack, left him feeling as though he had lost a friend. As Charles and Diana breakfasted together that morning, other reporters and photographers began to arrive in the village but none of us then knew of the horse's death. We had not followed the Prince on to the Downs, part of which is private, and it was an hour or two before news of the tragedy was relayed to us. The Prince, now very upset, left Lambourn with Diana, still intent that they should not be photographed together before the big day. They left in convoy, Prince Charles in the estate car, Lady Diana in the Land Rover with a Rover, carrying three police officers, bringing up the rear. Only days away from becoming engaged to the heir to the throne, Lady Diana lay on the muddy floor of the farm vehicle to avoid being photographed.

I believe that the tragedy over Allibar helped bring a change of plan that weekend. For there are reasons to think that the engagement day was brought forward at the last moment. We may never know, but several things point to the possibility that the announcement was originally scheduled to come several weeks later. That weekend, James Whitaker of the *Star* telephoned Lady Diana, who assured him she was returning to the kindergarten the following *Tuesday*. Prince Charles also had an engagement the same Tuesday, while several other dates were free throughout the month and into the next.

I believe that Prince Charles grew weary of the secrecy, and the clandestine meetings, regretful of the fact that Lady Diana should have to drive herself – sometimes hundreds of miles – whenever they wished to meet. It was certainly no way to treat a lady. The pressure was becoming intolerable, and it may be that Allibar's death was the last straw. Prince Charles wanted their romance brought out into the open, so that he could hold his head up and show his love for her, rather than hide it with subterfuge.

Cynics were later to claim that the engagement was timed to draw attention away from the disastrous unemployment figures due for realease that day – the jobless total had reached 2,463,294. But I cannot accept that the Prince would have allowed a political consideration to affect one of the happiest days in his life.

On the final weekend before the engagement – the last opportunity for any journalist to 'break' the story – I had been more concerned about a particular aspect of Allibar's

123

death. As the group of us had waited outside Mr Gaselee's home, we had laughed and talked among ourselves, mainly to keep our spirits up in the sub-zero temperature.

It occurred to me that the Prince must have thought us callous and uncaring if he believed we *knew* of the horse's death, and I decided to put the record straight, by telephoning Lady Diana.

James Whitaker, incidentally, had the same thought, except that in his case he decided to write a letter to Prince Charles personally. In view of the widely accepted belief then that the Press and the Royal Family were daggers-drawn the whole time, I should perhaps add that Prince Charles took the time to write a perfectly charming reply, in his own hand – *and dated 24 February*, which one might think was a busy day.

I put my call through to Lady Diana on the morning of Monday, the 23rd. Lady Diana was not there. When would she be back? 'I don't know.' Well, will she back tomorrow? 'Well, er, I'm not sure when she's coming back.' Lady Diana's flatmates were nothing if not honest, and the hesitancy in the voice was worrying.

The first faint feeling of unease began to creep into my mind. In the early afternoon came the first tip – from a source I obviously cannot name – that the engagement was to be announced the following morning. Vague rumours began to creep into other newspapers offices in Fleet Street, as I put through calls to several contacts, seeking confirmation.

It still seemed impossible. There had been so many rumours before. In the late afternoon, I decided to telephone Warwick Hutchins, Prince Charles' Press officer, for guidance. I told him of the tip I had received, and said I would be happy to kill the rumours on his say-so. Warwick played it by the book with a carefully worded reply: 'Announcements are made when they are made, Harry, and there is nothing further I can say to help you.'

'Warwick,' I replied, 'I'm not asking for a Board of Trade enquiry! Just tell me it's nonsense, and I'll forget it.'

'Announcements are made when they are made, Harry,

and there is nothing further I can say to help you,' he repeated.

'Warwick, you are making me nervous,' I said.

'Do you want me to say it again?' he asked. There was no need to. I could see he was not going to budge, but by now alarm bells were ringing in my ears.

Warwick had behaved perfectly correctly, but as one of the most civilized Press officers that Buckingham Palace has ever had, he would have been more helpful if he could have done. But his blank reply was a bigger clue than he knew. We were approaching the first edition deadline and it was time to consult my news editor, Tom Petrie. He sat up with a jolt when I told him what I suspected was about to happen. Was I sure enough to go into print, he wanted to know. It was a difficult question to answer.

After the *Daily Express* blunder over Princess Marie-Astrid years earlier, I could not afford to get it wrong – not even once. I had firmly nailed my journalistic colours to the mast that Lady Diana was the one – now was not the time to panic. But we were running out of time. The first and second editions came and passed. The call I was waiting for finally came through – from the original source – saying 'Yes, it looks as though it's on.'

I was now eighty-five per cent sure, but I hesitated. Then came the last – and most perfectly timed clue. Two photographers working for the *Sun* checked the where-abouts of Lady Diana's Mini Metro because of the information we had. Where should they find it, but parked bang on the forecourt of Buckingham Palace. That was all we needed. I immediately telephoned the Palace Press office and spoke this time to Miss Anne Wall. It will help those outside Fleet Street to judge just how difficult royal reporting can be when I say that Miss Wall told me there was nothing significant in Lady Diana being at the Palace.

'It is commonly known that Prince Charles and Lady Diana have been seeing each other for some time, so it would not altogether be surprising if she called at the Palace from time to time.' When I pressed the point, she said: 'I don't think I want to go on with this ridiculous conversation any longer.'

The engagement was then little more than twelve hours away.

'Nothing significant', 'Not surprising' – it did not add up.

What had happened was that Lady Diana had joined Prince Charles, the Queen and Prince Philip for dinner at the Palace on the eve of the announcement. She had moved some of her belongings out of her flat and stayed that night at Clarence House, the home of the Queen Mother. The protective arms of the Royal Family had closed around her.

To be fair to Miss Wall, it is perfectly possible that even then she did not know about the announcement. It was a closely guarded secret right up to the last moment. The conversation temporarily unnerved me, but there was no time left for hesitation. The third, and main edition deadline was approaching. It was now or never.

I telephoned the *Sun*'s copy room, where stories are taken down via headphones. I dictated my name and the 'catchline' – Lady Diana.

'That's the easy part,' I said. 'Now I've got to think how I'm going to say it.'

By 2 a.m. the *Sun* was on the streets with its world-exclusive picture story – 'Lady Di Goes to the Palace' – covering the whole of the front page and the centre pages. The *Sun* had gone out on a limb – and it did so boldly.

I was astonished later to see that *The Times* carried, with great style, a small story on its front page, calmly stating that the royal engagement was to be announced that day.

The story was the result of a leak from a high source. Earl Spencer had his own theory when he later said: 'Number Ten had to be told – 'nuff said.' He was presumably suggesting that a member of the staff in Downing Street, or a politician who had learned by chance, had passed on the information to *The Times*. However the leak came about, it required no effort on the part of *The Times*. We had *worked* for our exclusive. The rest of Fleet Street was left floundering. News desks work throughout the night and, when copies of the *Sun* 'dropped' in the early hours of the morning in newspaper offices throughout Fleet Street, there was uproar.

By breakfast-time every radio news bulletin said in its lead story: 'According to two newspapers, the *Sun* and *The Times*, Prince Charles is to announce his engagement today to Lady Diana Spencer. Buckingham Palace has refused to comment on the reports.' The only way the BBC and other radio stations could report the story at all was by saying what we were saying!

Even then, there were many in Fleet Street who believed we had got it wrong. With the rest of the nation that morning I held my breath.

# Chapter Ten

### 'Our Beloved Son'

AT 10 A.M. on Tuesday, 24 February 1981, Prince Charles was due at the Foreign and Commonwealth Office in Whitehall. The visit was part of his familiarization programme with the workings of government – a routine affair which would normally have attracted probably one rota photographer from Fleet Street. Today, the excitement engendered by the stories in the *Sun* and *The Times* caused every newspaper in Fleet Street to send a photographer and, in many cases, a writer as well. The large team of media men was joined by television crews, and a barrier had to be hastily set up to keep the situation orderly. Even at this late hour no one knew for certain what might happen but news desks were taking no chances.

Photographers and reporters gathered, too, outside Lady Diana's flat and at the kindergarten in Pimlico; of course, she was at neither place. Lady Diana was in Clarence House, trying on a royal blue, two-piece suit with a white blouse, decorated with a motif of blue swallows. At the Foreign Office, a member of the news department came outside, where by now hundreds of sightseers were gathering, and explained the programme for the Prince's visit. It was due to last three hours, he said. It seemed extraordinary that on this of all days, Prince Charles would have time for a three-hour tour. Perhaps the reports of an engagement announcement were totally wrong, people wondered. After all, the Prince had not been courting Lady Diana all that long. Perhaps the romance would end just as all the others had done. These were nervous moments.

At one minute *past* ten, I remarked to my colleague James Whitaker, 'Have you ever known Prince Charles to arrive late for an official engagement?'

At two minutes past ten, a senior official from the news department came outside to the waiting crowd and announced in a loud voice: 'The Prince of Wales has decided to postpone his visit.'

That was it! The Pressmen disappeared inside sixty seconds. The only place to go was to Buckingham Palace, where a crowd of several thousand waited outside the gates, in the freezing cold, hoping for dramatic developments. At 10.30 a.m. the Court correspondent of the BBC was summoned to the Palace. So, too was Grania Forbes, the Court correspondent of the Press Association news agency. Now was the moment. At 11 a.m. precisely, a newsflash went out on the tapes and into thousands of newspaper offices up and down the country. It read: 'Prince Charles to marry Lady Diana Spencer – official.'

Simultaneous announcements were broadcast as the lead item on the news bulletins of all the radio stations. And the details of the momentous news everyone had been waiting for were released in a Press Association story. But the working of a simple statement issued by Buckingham Palace said it all:

> It is with the greatest pleasure that the Queen and the Duke of Edinburgh announce the betrothal of their beloved son, the Prince of Wales, to the Lady Diana Spencer, daughter of the Earl Spencer and the Honourable Mrs Shand Kydd.

Mr Michael Shea, the Queen's Press secretary, told the Press Association: 'The wedding will be in the summer, but no precise date or place has been chosen.' He added: 'The Queen and the Duke of Edinburgh have both known Lady Diana Spencer for some time and are delighted at the engagement.'

As the announcement went out, the Queen was in the Palace ballroom for an investiture. She beamed with delight as the Lord Chamberlain, Lord Maclean, addressed the people waiting to receive awards.

There was a hush as he said: 'Her Majesty the Queen has

asked me to let you know that an announcement is being made at this moment in the following terms.' There was enthusiastic applause as he read the formal statement, and the Band of the Coldstream Guards struck up with the tune 'Congratulations'. Throughout the Palace, hundreds of bottles of pink champagne – the Prince's favourite – were being uncorked to celebrate the news. (Household staff, who had also been kept in the dark, had known it must be true when they had arrived for work to find that their office fridges had been filled with the bottles of bubbly.)

Prince Charles and Lady Diana, together in the Palace, could not contain their joy. Surrounded by young secretaries, they toasted each other with glasses of champagne, and Lady Diana proudly showed off her engagement ring. It was a beauty – a deep blue, oval sapphire, surrounded by fourteen diamonds and set in eighteen-carat white gold. It was made by Garrards, the Crown jewellers. Lady Diana did her best to hide her finger nails as she stretched out her left hand – she had been nibbling them in the excitement.

The couple gave their first interview about the engagement a few minutes later in the same sitting-room where their love had been sealed. But they had contained their feelings for each other for so long that, at first, the words would not come.

'Thrilled' was the only word both could think of to sum up their feelings, when they spoke to Grania Forbes of the Press Association. Grania was pretty thrilled herself. She had been on maternity leave when the Prince, who knows her well, said he would like her to conduct the first interview, and she had been hastily summoned from her home. Grania, an experienced reporter who has a way of instantly putting people at their ease, soon had Charles and Diana happily chatting about their feelings for each other.

The Prince spoke of the night he had proposed, of how he had asked Lady Diana to think it over. It was then that Lady Diana chipped in with, 'Oh I never had any doubts about it.' It was settled there and then, but the difficult part, said Prince Charles, was keeping the secret to themselves. They said their romance began when Lady Diana went to Balmoral the previous autumn.

'We began to realize then that there was something in it,' said Charles.

Although the couple had met in childhood neither could remember meeting before November 1977 – the year of the Queen's Silver Jubilee. Lady Diana said, Charles came to shoot and we met in the middle of a ploughed field. He was really a friend of my sister, Lady Sarah, then.'

Prince Charles said, 'I remember a very jolly and amusing and bouncy sixteen-year-old. She was very attractive. She was great fun and full of life.'

Lady Diana's first impression of the Prince was, she said, 'Pretty amazing'. As they spoke, the Prince, wearing a grey lounge suit, and Lady Diana a red velvet skirt and jacket with matching shirt, sat at opposite ends of a sofa. They exchanged glances, but Lady Diana was a little shy and left her fiancé to conduct most of the interview.

And another indication that the engagement had been brought forward came from the Prince's lips when he said that the decision was so recent that many plans for the future had not yet been finalized. They were still debating where the wedding would take place and where they should go on honeymoon. 'We have discussed vague ideas and now people might come up with suggestions of where we might go,' he said.

They had not decided where they would live after their honeymoon. 'I have only two rooms and a bedroom in Buckingham Palace so it will obviously be difficult to stay here for very long,' said the Prince.

Asked if she had got Highgrove organized, Lady Diana replied with a grin, 'Not quite, yet,' and the Prince added: 'It's just like camping. We've only got one room decorated downstairs and the bedroom organized. Otherwise everything is being painted. There's nothing there yet, no curtains, carpets or furniture – nothing.'

The Prince pointed out that they both loved the country and he would prefer to spend much time there. One thing on which both agreed – the twelve-year age-gap did not matter.

'I have never thought about the age-gap,' she said, and the Prince joked back: 'Diana will certainly keep me young – you are only as old as you think you are. But I shall be exhausted!'

He said he thought Lady Diana would make a 'very, very, good Princess of Wales'. And he had no doubts about her ability to cope with the official duties involved. 'She will be twenty soon and I was about that age when I started. It's obviously difficult to start with, but you just have to plunge in.'

Lady Diana was more cautious. 'I will take it as it comes,' she said.

The couple both thought they had a lot in common. 'Diana is a great outdoor-loving sort of person. She's a very energetic character as well,' he said.

Lady Diana said: 'We both love music and dancing and we both have the same sense of humour.'

'You'll definitely need that!' said the Prince with a laugh.

Like her sister Sarah, Lady Diana is a 'great skier', said the Prince. 'I was very cross at being left behind this spring,' she said, referring to the Klosters holiday.

Despite her shyness, Lady Diana seemed poised and confident as she sat beside the Prince, and she conceded that it was 'marvellous' to have his moral support. 'It's always nice when there are two of you and there's someone there to help you.' she said.

They repeated their favourite word for the way they felt as the interview drew to a close – 'Thrilled'. And in love? 'Of course,' said Lady Diana, while the cautious Prince added: 'Whatever "in love" means.'

At the end of the interview, the Prince thanked Grania and asked when her baby was due. It was then only a few weeks away and Grania, knowing that several royal births were imminent, joked: 'I'm leading the field.' The Prince laughed and wished her luck with the birth.

Grania dashed off to the telephone, feverishly reading

through her notes. 'I had no tape-recorder with me, and I had to take it all down in shorthand,' she said later. 'It was difficult to do that as well as ask the questions and look at Prince Charles and Lady Diana. It was an interview to remember. But it was a typically kind thought of the Prince to ask for me personally, knowing how I had traipsed behind him for four years.'

Lady Diana gave a clear indication of her fashion-consciousness by choosing bright red stockings and shoes to match her velvet outfit for the interview with Grania. But for the television interview which followed, Lady Diana – knowing it would be in colour – changed into the blue outfit she had bought specially for the occasion. She knew the colour suited her – and it went well with the sapphire ring.

Prince Charles and Lady Diana walked proudly arm-in-arm on the terrace and lawns behind Buckingham Palace for the television interviews and the 'photo-call' with Press Association photographer Ron Bell, shooting black and white, and Tim Graham taking colour.

Tim, who at last had the picture in his viewfinder that he had been trying to get for months, waited until they were both smiling then pressed the motor-drive button of his Nikon, giving the couple what is referred to in Fleet Street as 'the whole roll'. Then he did the same with two other cameras. As the film raced through the cameras – thirty-six frames in less than fifteen seconds – Lady Diana giggled and told him: 'You're just showing off.' In fact, every single frame was developed within hours of Tim leaving the Palace – and the pictures went round the world.

Prince Charles later selected one of Tim's shots as his favourite and placed a huge order to give to his friends and relatives.

Facing the television cameras, Prince Charles joked about the problems Press coverage had given him. While Lady Diana was in Australia, he said, 'I rang up on one occasion and they said she was not taking any calls. Other people had telephoned saying they were me – with Australian accents. I said, "It's the Prince of Wales speaking," but they said,

"How do we know it's the Prince of Wales?" and I said, "You don't but I am."' Eventually, he had to telephone another number before he was able to speak to his bride-to-be.

The Prince spoke again of how they fell in love. 'It was gradual,' he said. 'I suppose it was towards the end of the summer and the autumn last year. I began to realize what was going through my mind and hers in particular. These things happen – it was a gradual business.'

Of their engagement, he said: 'We have had to sit on it for three weeks which hasn't been easy. I was determined it was going to be a secret.'

They both laughed when they were told that Lady Diana's father had just said she would make a good housewife. 'That remains to be seen,' laughed Prince Charles.

Lady Diana was asked how she felt about the responsibilities of being married to the future king. 'Naturally, it is quite daunting,' she said. 'I hope it won't be too difficult. I have had a run up to it all in the last six months and I hope I've coped. With Charles beside me, I can't go wrong. I am very much looking forward to meeting lots of different people.'

Did she like travelling? 'I'm going to have to,' she said with a giggle. In a moment of undisguised affection, Lady Diana laid her head on the Prince's shoulder as he concluded expressing his feelings by saying: 'I am amazed she has been brave enough to take me on. I am delighted and happy.'

Then – in his usual style – he ended with a joke: he apologized for missing his appointment at the Foreign Office, and said with a laugh: 'I have always wanted to throw a spanner in the works of my programme – I think I have managed to throw in a crowbar.'

The couple walked arm-in-arm back into the Palace to continue their celebration, and throughout the country more bottles of champagne were uncorked by friends, well-wishers and people who were simply delighted for them. The announcement brought, as much as anything, a tremendous feeling of relief among thousands of people. When a television team stopped people in the street to tell them the

134

news and seek their reactions, the first man they approached said. 'Thank goodness!'

And with the secret out, a veritable flood-gate of joy opened among the handful who had been in on it – and among those who wanted to add their own congratulations. Outside the Palace, the crowd cheered and clapped as the news filtered through.

Television teams were erecting platforms for outside broadcast units, and the traffic came to a standstill as drivers craned to see what was going on. In the middle of it all, Earl Spencer arrived in his gold-coloured Rolls Royce, not to go inside but to see the historic scene for himself and savour the carnival atmosphere.

With him were his wife, Raine, and her twelve-year-old son, Henry, and the family were clearly enjoying themselves. A beaming Lord Spencer, who carried a Leicaflex camera, declared: 'We came here because I wanted to photograph the photographers. I have photographed every important event in Diana's life, and I wanted to record this one as well.' The proud father went on:

> Diana is a giver, not a taker. She was always a delightful child, and as a baby she could have won any beauty competition. Publicity doesn't worry her. She'll take it all in her stride. She's very practical and down to earth, and a very good housewife. When I told Charles the same thing, he said, 'I know', and Charles is very lucky to have her. We had drinks with the two of them at the Palace last night and Diana was looking radiant and happy but a bit nervous.

He revealed that Prince Charles had telephoned him to ask for Lady Diana's hand in marriage. 'I wonder what he would have done if I had said "No",' chuckled the Earl. He went on: 'I'm so happy that all this is out in the open. It's been a very difficult time for us and even more difficult for Diana. The Royal Family loves Di – and the two of them just want to be together.' Then he added what everyone knew: 'I'm so excited about all this I could burst!'

135

Lady Spencer, wearing a white mink coat and matching hat, joined in with glowing praise for her stepdaughter. 'She'd got a marvellous, even temperament,' she said. 'She's not at all the sort of person to get highly strung or depressed.'

Lady Spencer said she guessed that, earlier in the year, Diana was in love with Prince Charles. 'Call it intuition if you like, but I just knew it. She was so very happy.'

She revealed that Diana had turned to them for a shoulder to lean on in the weeks leading up to the announcement. 'We tried to provide a refuge from all the personal problems. She had to think over a very momentous decision,' she said. 'Di was terribly anxious to do the right thing and not to say too much.' Lady Spencer reflected her stepdaughter's remarkably harmonious relationship with royal reporters when she said: 'Di has got on well with the Press over the last few months. The newspaper people did their utmost to be wonderful and kind to her and she liked them for that.'

Lady Spencer, too, had found it hard to keep the secret. 'We've been bursting to tell people,' she said. 'Now I just feel on top of the world.'

Back at Old Brompton Road, where the flat was to go up for sale only twenty-four hours later, Lady Diana's flatmates shared their excitement with the rest of the world. And they revealed that Lady Diana had burst into tears the night she told them of her wedding plans. Virginia Pitman, a twenty-one-year-old cookery student who was at school with Lady Diana, recalled:

> Di just sat on the bed beside me and said she was going to marry Prince Charles. There was a big smile on her face. We started to squeal with excitement and then we started to cry. We have known about the romance for a long time but we have never met Prince Charles. He never came to the flat.
>
> We are all thrilled for Di and looking forward to seeing the engagement ring.

Carolyn Pride, a nineteen-year-old student at the Royal

College of Music, told how she was 'in the loo' when Lady Diana broke the news.

> There was a lot of shouting and we all burst into tears. It was all very emotional. We knew about the engagement soon after Prince Charles proposed. But it wasn't hard to keep the secret. We never dreamed of telling anyone. It's not the kind of thing one does to one's friends. We have been ever so discreet – that's the way we were brought up. We had a celebration breakfast the morning after Di told us the news. It was a really jolly meal. We were all so thrilled.

Lady Diana had also told her friends that, when she was younger, Prince Charles had treated her like a kid sister, and that she has a signed copy of the fairy-tale book he wrote for his brothers – *The Old Man of Lochnagar*.

The engagement announcement carried with it a tinge of sadness for the three girls who had lived together through a unique period in Lady Diana's life – and British royal history. Said Virginia: 'We're great, great friends, and we're sticking together as long as possible.'

Not only the three flatmates but many other people kept the secret for varying lengths of time, and it seems amazing in retrospect that not a single one gave it away. The whole band of the Coldstream Guards must have had a good idea what was going on the night before when they were told to rehearse 'Congratulations'.

And Lady Diana's 'boss' knew as well. At the kindergarten, where the children gathered round the radio at 11 a.m. to hear the announcement about 'Miss Diana', the headmistress Vicky Wilson revealed she had known on the Monday night. Lady Diana had telephoned her from Buckingham Palace sounding 'thrilled' but very relaxed about it all. Mrs Wilson went on: 'She said that the wedding and her new role as the Princess of Wales would make it impossible to continue working here. We shall all miss her very much.'

'The children will miss her too. Lady Diana loves children and I am sure she will make a wonderful mother.'

After the radio announcement, the children went quiet for a moment – then started chatting away, she said. Some were too young to understand, while others recorded the occasion by painting their idea of how Lady Diana and Prince Charles would look on their wedding day. But even those who did not realize that the 'lovely lady' was to become part of the Royal Family remembered the times she danced in the hall with them, helped them with their paintings and joined in the games.

While the children carried on playing, the staff slipped into the kitchen and celebrated with champagne – drunk out of coffee mugs.

Up in Grantham, Lincolnshire, the Prince's 'old flame', Lady Diana's sister, Lady Sarah McCorquodale, was over the moon.

'I'm Cupid. I introduced them,' she said delightedly. 'It's a perfect match – they are made for each other.'

Lady Diana had phoned her sister from her West Kensington hairdressers at 9 a.m. that morning, sounding 'very excited'. Said Lady Sarah: 'She was in seventh heaven. I phoned Charles to congratulate him – he is so happy.'

She was certain she said that the couple were made for each other.

> He met Miss Right and she met Mr Right. They just clicked. They will be totally compatible in marriage. They have the same sense of humour – she's giggly and so is he. She loves ballet, opera and sport, and so does he. I think she will make a wonderful Princess of Wales.'

Lady Sarah said she realized her sister was in love just before Christmas.

> There was an extra sparkle in her eyes. Then about ten days ago I saw her at her flat and she was totally radiant – bouncing, bubbling. I said, 'You're engaged', and she admitted it.'

Of her own friendship with the Prince, she added: 'It was never a romance – always platonic. I told the world that but no one believed me.'

As thousands of telegrams of congratulations began to pour into Buckingham Palace, the London Post Office found themselves overwhelmed. By late afternoon, callers to Inland Telegrams were told: 'We can't promise that it will get there in the next couple of days.' (Earl Spencer, alone, received more than 1000.)

Naturally, it turned out that Lady Diana had been in love with the Prince since she was eleven years old. Miss Ruth Rudge, principal of Lady Diana's old school in Sevenoaks, said that Diana slept with a picture of the Prince above her bed in the school dormitory.

And old Etonian Simon Berry, who was among a party of eighteen – including Lady Diana – who spent a two-week holiday in the French Alps in 1979, remembered the day that Lady Diana hinted that she might one day walk down the aisle with Prince Charles. 'We were discussing the future and I asked Diana what she wanted to do,' said Simon. 'She replied "I would love to be a successful dancer – or maybe the Princess of Wales".'

It was Simon who revealed a hitherto unknown side of Lady Diana.

> She likes watching *Crossroads* on television, and does a fantastic impersonation of Miss Piggy of *The Muppets*. She has a great deal in common with ordinary people and it won't be difficult for her to carry out her duties as the Princess of Wales – and hopefully, one day, as Queen of England. She has a wonderful gift for getting on well with everybody. She will not be weighed down by all the red tape.

He remembered, too, how 'Di' had to almost fight off would-be boyfriends.

> She has broken the hearts of dozens of young men. Chaps would meet her and instantly fall in love. Many have tried to win her – sending her flowers and begging for a date. But she always politely declined. Diana is a

fabulous girl. What a lucky man Prince Charles is –
there is simply no way he could resist her.

The warm mood which swept the nation that bitterly cold
Tuesday bubbled over into the City of London. Shares rode
high on the prospect of a rich summer and in the words of an
ancient rhyme:

*Among our ancient markets,*
*And in the City's Walls,*
*So many shares re-echoed,*
*God Bless the Prince of Wales.*

The shares of Royal Worcester, Wedgwood, and
Staffordshire potteries shot up with the anticipation of huge
orders for commemorative mugs and plates. For
Wedgwood, the announcement was seen by the staff as a life-
raft. They had been on a three-day week for several months,
but knew by midday that they would be quickly returning to
a four- or five-day week.

The tourist and hotel trades were jubilant at the prospect
of tens of thousands of extra tourists pouring into London,
and major West End stores began gearing up their buying
departments without delay.

Birmingham Mint shares soared at the thought of all those
lovely coins they would be minting. Incredibly, Royal
Wedding medallions would be on sale within twenty-four
hours, they said – though they denied receiving an 'early
warning' – and they planned a limited edition of one hundred
gold medallions at a mere £598 apiece.

Even brewery shares shot up at the prediction that
celebration toasts in every beverage from champagne to beer
would last right up to the wedding and beyond.

At one London hotel, a royal engagement cocktail was
instantly created and went on sale at £3.00 a glass, while an
enterprising baker at Melsham, Wiltshire, swiftly cooked
heart-shaped doughnuts bearing the initials 'C' and 'D'
which sold like hot cakes.

*The Archers* radio programme – dearly loved by millions –

signed off with the song 'Some Day My Prince Will Come', instead of its usual signature tune.

It was, all in all, quite a day for the country and still the congratulations poured in. The Archbishop of Canterbury who had been told earlier that he would officiate at the wedding, was the first to congratulate the couple. He announced the engagement at the General Synod of the Church of England during a debate – appropriately – on marriage. After the prolonged applause he said: 'I am sure the Synod will want to express its happiness at the news of the royal engagement and send our best wishes to the Prince of Wales and Lady Diana.'

The Prime Minister, Mrs Margaret Thatcher, revealed she had been told by the Queen on the Monday morning, and she in turn informed some of her senior ministers. In the House of Commons, MPs cheered as she spoke of the 'great pleasure' the news brought; Lord Hailsham, the Lord Chancellor, and David Steel, leader of the Liberal Party, added their own best wishes.

In Australia, the Prime Minister, Mr Malcolm Fraser, interrupted a debate in the House of Representatives in Canberra to break the news, and Lieutenant Roy Clare, the commanding officer of Prince Charles' former ship HMS *Bronington*, sent a congratulatory signal to his old 'shipmate'.

The village of Doughton, in which Highgrove stands, celebrated the event by placing a red carpet in its only telephone box, and in nearby Tetbury, Union Jacks were hoisted.

On radio stations, the old Paul Anka hit 'Diana' found a new lease of life, with its telling line: 'You're so young, and I'm so old – this my darling I've been told.' Associated Television dropped the biggest clanger of the day: after mentioning Lady Diana they flashed a picture of Lady Jane Wellesley on the screen. The red-faced presenter, Bob Warman, said: 'All we can say is sorry . . .'

Prince Charles' last love before Lady Diana chipped in with best wishes. Anna Wallace broke her long silence on the

141

Prince to say: 'I am very happy for them. I think it's wonderful news. I think Lady Diana will make a very good Queen. She's very dignified and discreet.' But Anna said she was not expecting an invitation to the wedding! She also offered some advice to the future Princess of Wales: 'Be totally devoted to your husband.'

Comedian Harry Secombe, one of the stars of the late-lamented radio programme *The Goon Show* – Prince Charles' favourite as a boy – added some advice of his own. 'Charles must keep his sense of humour at all times,' he said, 'especially when he's changing the nappies.'

At the end of Charles' and Diana's special day, they celebrated with an engagement party at Clarence House, and a crowd of well-wishers who sang 'Congratulations' outside received a special treat. Prince Charles and Lady Diana emerged, hand-in-hand at the end of the evening. Charles, in black dinner suit, and Diana, wearing a white silk blouse and a red satin skirt, happily posed for amateur photographers. The only person who missed the wedding fever was Lady Diana's mother, Mrs Shand Kydd. 'She's stuck in Australia,' said the Prince.

The only discordant note struck on a day of celebration came from arch anti-royalist MP Willie Hamilton, who said the engagement date had been decided on by the Prime Minister and Buckingham Palace to hide the unemployment figures. He added, sourly: 'After the wedding there will be months of speculation as to when she is going to have a baby. It's all mush.'

But nobody was listening. This was a day the country wanted to remember with happiness.

The following day, after the heady atmosphere of the celebrations, Prince Charles and Lady Diana returned to more mundane matters. The Prince clinched a deal for a new racehorse, Good Prospect, to replace Allibar, while Diana returned to her flat to start collecting together some of her belongings. As she did so, her mother flew into Heathrow from Australia.

The announcement, of course, had come as no surprise,

'but I am absolutely delighted,' she said and added: 'I enormously approve of my daughters marrying the men they love.'

Of her daughter's future she said: 'It's an unknown world for her, but I'm sure she can cope and learn very quickly. She will have enormous support from her husband. I am sure she will manage.'

The morning-after-the-night-before brought for Lady Diana the first taste of her new lifestyle. And for all its privileges, she quickly discovered the drawbacks too. She could no longer nip around London at will in her Mini Metro, and when she returned to her flat, she was accompanied for the first time by a full-time bodyguard. The man appointed to protect her was Chief Inspector Paul Officer, a burly six-footer who for many years had been part of the Prince's security team. He is widely regarded as the man who saved Prince Charles' life during an incident in 1974 while the Prince was serving in the Royal Navy. The Prince was asleep in the naval barracks at Portland, Dorset, when another lieutenant, with a history of mental illness, went berserk with a knife. He broke into the Prince's private quarters and was confronted by the Prince himself who had been awakened by the noise. The demented officer was about to bring a chair crashing down on the Prince's head when Chief Inspector Officer rushed into the room and wrestled the assailant to the ground. Prince Charles never forgot the incident, and it was a measure of his concern for the safety of his bride-to-be that he asked for Officer to be assigned to her.

Lady Diana quickly found royal protection restrictive, but she nevertheless asserted her independence of spirit. When the detective complained about the activities of a particular Fleet Street photographer, she insisted: 'But I like him.'

As details of the wedding began to emerge it became clear that Prince Charles was determined to do it 'my way'.

November is a favourite date for royal weddings, but in the past loyal crowds have often had to wait many hours in the cold and drizzle for the spectacle. Prince Charles chose 29

July, the height of summer. And instead of Westminster Abbey, the recent choice for royal weddings, he decided upon St Paul's Cathedral, because it could seat several hundred more guests.

The Dean of St Paul's, the Very Rev. Alan Webster, was swift to promise 'a holy and homely feeling amid the grandeur – a village wedding in the presence of millions of viewers through television'.

The Prince's decision also meant that the wedding procession – one of the last great state occasions this century – would take a slightly longer route, along the Strand and Fleet Street and up Ludgate Hill, compared with the 'short-cut' of Whitehall to the Abbey.

The choice of St Paul's was an historic one, for the last Prince of Wales to be married there was Prince Arthur, Henry VII's eldest son, who married Catherine of Aragon in 1501. But that was in the old cathedral which was destroyed in the Great Fire of London. The wedding would, in any case, be surrounded by history. In choosing an English bride, the Prince broke a 300-year run of 'imports'. Lady Diana was to be the first 'home-grown' bride for an heir to the throne since 1659.

The last had been Anne Hyde, elder daughter of the first Earl of Clarendon, who married the Duke of York, later King James II. English brides before her included four of the six wives of Henry VIII, more than a century earlier. The present Queen Mother was Lady Elizabeth Bowes-Lyon, daughter of the Scottish Earl of Strathmore, when she married the future King George VI.

King George V had married Princess Mary, daughter of the German Duke of Teck, and his predecessor, Edward VII, married a Danish princess, eldest daughter of King Christian IX of Denmark. Even Queen Victoria had taken a foreign partner, marrying the German Prince Albert, and all her Hanoverian ancestors, from William IV and George IV back to George I in 1714, had married German princesses.

Lady Diana is an English rose indeed.

As Mr Harold Brooks-Baker, managing director of

*Debrett's Peerage*, put it: 'She will bring back Stuart blood to the Royal Family. She descends five times from Charles II – four times on the wrong side of the blanket, and one on the right side.' (The witty and bawdy king was notorious for his prolific love-life which produced innumerable illegitimate children.) With so much doubtful history behind them, it would seem that the Royal couple could only improve on it.

Within twenty-four hours of their engagement, Prince Charles and Lady Diana began to actively plan their wedding. The Royal Yacht *Britannia* was ordered to be on stand-by for the honeymoon – and the Prince consulted his family about the ceremony itself.

To say that it was planned, from the outset, as the wedding of the century is not to downgrade the Queen's own ceremony. That took place in 1947 in the aftermath of World War II – she even had to save her clothing coupons for the wedding dress. The Queen, as the loving mother she is, gave orders that no effort should be spared to make this wedding one of the greatest spectacles of modern times.

On the first weekend of their engagement, the couple were guests of the Marquis of Cholmondeley, at his castle home in Cheshire. Sixty-one-year-old Lord Cholmondeley holds the ancient title of Lord Great Chamberlain of England, and is the man responsible for much of the pomp and ceremony of royal occasions. His help was invaluable in deciding the venue for the wedding and planning the procession route. The couple spent hours discussing their plans with him during their break in the country. Lord Cholmondeley told me: 'I was glad to offer the Prince and Lady Diana whatever assistance I could.' Prince Charles also found time to put in a spot of hunting, and on the Sunday they attended a service in the private chapel on the Cholmondeley estate.

The Prince appropriately chose St David's Day – celebrating the patron saint of Wales – to take his bride-to-be to Church for the first time. I was the only reporter in the church, among a congregation of less than twenty people, and the Prince and Lady Diana nodded a friendly welcome, Then they knelt side by side as the Vicar of Cholmondeley,

Rev. Peter Roberts, offered a prayer for young couples about to marry:

> Grant that the hopes and dreams in their hearts may be fulfilled;
>
> Draw them ever closer to one another and to Thee;
>
> Give them the grace to bear one another's burdens and share one another's joys;
>
> And grant that they may live together in faithful love until their lives end. Amen.

The words were simple but moving, and there was no mistaking the look of love in the eyes of Prince Charles and Lady Diana as they said their first prayer together, and looked towards their betrothal with hope and faith.

Back in London on the Monday morning, Lady Diana began to think how she could match the Prince's long-standing 'Action Man' image for innovation, imagination and sheer nerve. At the same time, Palace advisers were deciding when the future Princess of Wales would make her public debut.

'Shy Di', with devilment in her heart, decided to make it an occasion to remember.

# Chapter Eleven

### 'Whatever Happened to Shy Di?'

As COMING-OUT parties go, Lady Diana could hardly have come out any further. The dress she wore for her first official engagement with Prince Charles plunged so low it looked in danger of never stopping. It was a stunner. A crowd of about one hundred people, who had braved the rain and cold outside the City of London's Goldsmith's Hall, gasped when she stepped out of a Rolls Royce, holding one hand protectively across her front. Millions more watched it on the television news that evening, and one designer called it 'the best cliff-hanger on TV since "Who Shot JR?"'

For a start, the dress was stark black, strapless and made of glossy silk taffeta. Worn with a simple diamond necklace and matching earrings, the effect was devastating. Photographers, who had flown into London from all over Europe for the occasion, outnumbered the public and as Lady Diana slipped a black stole from her shoulders, she was illuminated in a blaze of flashlights. She giggled, and Prince Charles – clearly enjoying the attention his bride-to-be was receiving – eyed the size of the Press contingent, and said with a laugh: 'It looks like a three-line whip tonight!'

The couple obligingly posed for a minute or two, and a City office worker, Miss Pamela Elkins, stepped from the crowd and handed Lady Diana a single pink rose. The colour could hardly have been better chosen by a whole committee of artists. With it was a card saying: 'To a lovely lady – an English Rose.'

Lady Diana shyly accepted it with a blush that matched the colour of the bloom. And she laughed again when the Prince asked, with a grin: 'Have all the fashion writers finished?' Then he proudly ushered her into the reception.

The occasion had been carefully chosen by Buckingham

Palace for Lady Diana's public debut. The evening of verse and music in aid of the Royal Opera House Development Fund had the advantage of being both glamorous and in support of a worthy cause. And it was known in advance that among the guests would be Princess Grace of Monaco. A former beauty herself, the Princess's fading charm was no match for the spring-fresh radiance of Lady Diana who stole the show. Lady Diana greeted the Princess with a graceful curtsy as protocol demanded, but there was little doubt who upstaged who. Prince Charles was less formal, as befitted his royal status, and he kissed the former film star on the cheek.

Lady Diana, taking her first dainty steps into high society, followed a pace or two behind the Prince as they circulated among the guests, and there were some who thought Prince Charles was inattentive towards her. But there was an air, too, of studied casualness about the Prince, as though he were jerking a metaphorical thumb over his shoulder with the proprietorial message to the other men present: 'The Lady belongs to me.' Deep down he was as pleased as Punch.

There was only one moment when Lady Diana's lack of experience of such occasions showed through. As she ascended a sweeping staircase, a television camera above her recording every move, she had difficulty in avoiding tripping over her dress. She kept her eyes down, concentrating on the voluminous folds, and it was only at the last moment that she glanced up and spotted the camera above her. She laughed as though to say, 'Oh, I didn't realize you were there,' but the moment was lost in the overall success of her 'performance'.

She ended the evening ahead. And her estimation in the eyes of the public rose by a marked degree. There was no doubt that, for a girl supposed to be shy and reserved, Lady Diana could be decidedly extrovert – not to say, sexy – when she wanted to be.

The newspapers had a field day the following morning. 'Di's Daring Debut', headlined one. 'Diana, the Dazzler', said another, and she was likened to both a blossoming rose and Scarlett O'Hara.

148

*That* dress became *the* talking point for days. Men raved about it. Women envied it. And photographs of it went around the world. The *New York Post* covered its front page with a head-and-shoulders picture, captioned: 'London Ayes The Royal Blush.'

The French, who know a beautiful lady when they see one, were full of praise. The Paris evening paper, *France-Soir*, said that Lady Diana had 'caused a sensation and her dress drew admiring "ohs" from the elegant gathering.' The report added lyrically: 'In her bright taffeta gown, it was clear that Diana held all the trumps . . . the future King of England is a very lucky man.'

In Australia, the *Melbourne Herald* said she had 'stunned London.' Only the cold-hearted Germans raised objections. The *Hamburg Abendblatt* untruthfully told its readers it was 'the dress that shocked England'.

But the gasps which greeted Lady Diana's entrance into her fiancés world were not out of shock for the daring of her *décolletage*, but out of admiration for her sheer style. Lady Diana had not only the figure to wear the dress, but the confidence too.

It took the fashion world by storm, and copies of it were in the shops within forty-eight hours. London designer Jeff Banks said: 'It was an exciting mixture of daring and panache. I was quite stunned when I saw it.' Internationally renowned Mary Quant thought it was 'terrific, absolutely beautiful and so romantic'.

The dress was designed by the husband and wife team of David and Elizabeth Emanuel, and such was the excitement it caused that the following morning Buckingham Palace was precipitated into ending the speculation over who would design the wedding dress by announcing that the honour would go to the same couple.

There were a few sour-pusses who claimed the design was old-fashioned. Indeed, the Queen and Princess Margaret both wore similar creations back in the Fifties. But Lady Diana proved that the fashion was back – or alternatively that there is no such thing as 'fashion', only taste. She also demonstrated that she was determined to bring a style of her own to the role of Princess of Wales.

Not for Lady Diana the safeness of a wedding day creation from the likes of the late Sir Norman Hartnell, who designed the Queen's wedding dress, although the old master himself would have approved of Lady Diana's 'little black number', according to his colleague George Mitchieson. Said Mr Mitchieson: 'He would have loved it. The off-the-shoulder look was one of his favourite lines. The evening dresses he designed for the Queen and Princess Margaret were also cut very low.'

Lady Diana chose the young Emanuel team – twenty-seven-year-old Liz and David who is twenty-eight – for a royal commission which catapulted them to the top of the fashion world. Their list of clients, which already included Princess Michael of Kent, the Duchess of Kent, Bianca Jagger and actress Jane Seymour, now had a new leader.

Lady Diana's curtsy to Princess Grace was a temporary but necessary precurser to the privilege and status she would enjoy after her wedding. As the wife of the heir to the throne, she will be expected to curtsy only to the Queen, the Queen Mother and – eventually – to the King himself.

From the beginning, Lady Diana put her own stamp of authority on how her lifestyle would progress, but not without the considerable advice of the Royal Family's most experienced and considerate expert in the art of simply being royal: the Queen Mother. From the night before the engagement, when she was taken under the wing of the Queen Mother at Clarence House, the grooming of Lady Diana began.

No princess-in-waiting could have asked for a better tutor. The Queen Mother had learned from bitter experience how it felt to be hurled headlong from a life of relative, but comfortable, obscurity into the revealing limelight of the throne. Her husband had been only the Duke of York when they had married, and they had no reason to foresee the trick which fate could play on their lives with the abdication of his brother. But it was her strength which helped George VI rise so magnificently to the occasion and become the popular king he was. Just as the Duke of York was not ready for it, so nothing in the life of Elizabeth Bowes-Lyon had prepared her for the demands of becoming Queen Consort to the King. The Queen Mother not only invented the art of 'becoming' royal, she perfected it to a degree which has never been matched.

The British constitutional historian Lord Blake wrote: 'The British monarchy has been one of the few success stories in British twentieth-century history. Amid economic and political decline, the dissolution of the Empire, and the exhausting struggles of two terrible wars it has stood out as a monument of stability.'

The Queen Mother has been a pillar of that monument. Once Prince Charles had made up his mind, she took on the task of preparing Lady Diana for the life she must lead, the rules she must learn, the mistakes she must never make. Lady Diana would be helped, too, by the other leading ladies of the Royal Family, notably Princess Anne and Princess Margaret, and she would no doubt study the popularity of such figures as the Duchess of Kent and Princess Alexandra. But it was from the Queen Mother that the nineteen-year-old beginner would learn the poise and artistry of regal behaviour. Certainly, she could not have done it alone.

When Prince Charles said, in his twenties, that 'the one advantage of marrying a princess or somebody from a royal family is that they do know what happens,' he was only half right. For it can hardly be supposed that a foreign princess, royally educated though she might be, would know the intimate workings of a British state occasion. How far less could an Earl's daughter be expected to have the knowledge of a British-born princess?

When Princess Anne married Captain Mark Phillips in Westminster Abbey, she whispered tips to him as they walked down the aisle. 'Don't forget to turn and ac-knowledge the Queen and the Duke of Edinburgh,' she murmured. But Lady Diana would, hopefully not need such last-minute coaching if the Queen Mother was to be successful in the task she had set herself.

There was more, however, in the grooming of Lady Diana than merely passing to her hints on how to behave on her wedding day. Brought up as she was in one of the great stately homes of England, Lady Diana already had the best manners and breeding the British aristocracy could provide.

But joining the Royal Family – revered throughout not only the Commonwealth but most of the civilized world – was a different matter. Lady Diana would have to learn to plan her life a year in advance, to gently 'drop' any friends who might cause her embarrassment, through their political or social connections; and at least learn to live with other acquaintances who might not normally be her natural choice of friends. Most urgently, she would have to acquire the skill of meeting strangers, of putting them at their ease, of thinking of something to say. To walk into a reception for, say, a diplomat from Uruguay and find a word for each of perhaps fifty guests, is a skill not easily developed. But at least in that instance there would be time to brush up on the geographical makeup and recent developments of that country. Harder still is the art of walking over to a face in the crowd, during a royal walk-about, and breaking the ice with a pertinent remark. The Queen, Prince Philip and the Queen Mother are all past masters at it.

There was much more for Lady Diana to learn. Refreshing though her sense of humour might be, she would have to restrain from giggling and keep a straight face when curtsied to by guests, even if they did happen to be her former flatmates or members of her own family. And, however kind her intentions, she would have to distance herself from household servants – treating them with civility but command – and adapt herself to accepting, without question, the greeting each day of 'Good morning, Your Royal Highness'. Royal etiquette demands nothing less.

As the future mistress of Highgrove, a particularly daunting role lay ahead. Guests arriving at the home of the Prince of Wales would expect something special in the way of hospitality and comfort. The setting of a dinner table, the choice of menu, the wines served and the compatibility of the table-guests would all be crucial: and the success or otherwise of the Prince's soirées would largely rest with his wife. In this, Lady Diana would be guided by watching the Queen Mother's own sure hand at arranging and stage-managing Clarence House dinner parties: by observing how she greeted her guests, how she would graciously overcome a particular guest's nervousness and how a hostess should subtly signify when a dinner party should come to an end.

In all these things, the Queen Mother was a persuasive but sympathetic teacher and during the four-and-half months between her engagement and her wedding, Lady Diana listened carefully to all she was told. Lady Diana did not always get it right first time. On Friday the 13th of March – an ill-omened date for both of them as it transpired – Lady Diana accompanied Prince Charles to Sandown Park, where he entered his new horse, Good Prospect, in the Horse and Hound Grand Military Gold Cup. While the Queen Mother and Princess Margaret wore sensible flat-heeled shoes, Lady Diana wore court shoes and, when she tried to walk around the parade ring, the spiky heels sank deep into the turf. Lady Diana tried to hide her mistake by walking on tip-toe, but it was no use. For any ordinary racegoer it would not have mattered in the slightest, but Lady Diana knew that a million eyes were watching on television screens throughout the country and it was a mistake she would not make again.

On that, her second public appearance since the engage-ment, the Queen Mother could be seen occasionally placing a reassuring hand on her shoulder. Later the three royal ladies were watching through binoculars when the Prince took a particularly bad fall at the eighteenth fence.

Lady Diana bit her lip and leapt to her feet in anxiety; and Princess Margaret in one swift, deft movement changed seats to be at her side. Fortunately, the Prince escaped with little more than a bloody nose, but had he been seriously hurt, Lady Diana would have needed immediate comfort. And Princess Margaret, no stranger herself to unhappiness, would have helped her from breaking down in public. Lady Diana Spencer was in good hands.

Lady Diana attended her first state banquet at Buckingham Palace a few days later and she was so nervous she could hardly eat. State banquets are glittering occasions and the grandeur is enough to test the nerve of any guest not totally familiar with royal protocol. For Lady Diana, it was made doubly difficult by the fact that every guest was dying for a close look at her. Prince Charles tried to 'protect' her by carefully placing her between himself and his cousin, the Duke of Gloucester, on the top table, knowing that the affable Duke would try to help her relax. But Lady Diana, dressed stunningly again in a low cut pale-blue gown with diamond necklace, bracelet and earrings, felt as if the eyes of the whole room were upon her. When the main course was served, she ignored the fillet of beef, and picked at the spinach, courgettes and side salad. It was a natural reaction, but Lady Diana would become accustomed in time to being the centre of attraction wherever she went.

As the months passed, and she became more and more a member of the Royal Family, the most difficult lesson she had to learn – but an essential one for her future role – was that of deliberately making herself remote from ordinary people. For the survival of the monarchy rests on the nation's deep-felt *need* for a Royal Family, a desire for them to be untouchable and larger-than-life. And the Royal Family themselves have reacted in modern times by deliberately cultivating their romantic image. Prince Charles has not been called a 'superstar' for nothing. The cloth-cap concept of bicycle-riding Royals may work in other countries, but Britain's remains uniquely different. In a sense the image is an illusion, for at the end of the day the Royal Family are human beings just like anyone else. The magic and the mystique of the monarchy has to be carefully nurtured, and, where necessary, embroidered. The 'royal wave' – so often the butt of satirists – is essentially a part of the Royal Family's *modus operandi*. Faintly ridiculous though it might sometimes look, the subjects of the monarch would feel disappointed, and perhaps cheated if it were ever replaced with a cheerful 'thumbs-up' signal. Within a few days of her engagement, Lady Diana could be seen giving her first hesitant royal wave as she was driven out of Buckingham Palace – although her hand was held the wrong way round. (The back of the hand must always be towards the crowd.)

But to deliberately hold oneself above the people was for Lady Diana, with her friendly outgoing nature, an altogether more unnatural stance. Without it, the Royal Family would become, well, everyday. Familiarity, in the case of the Royals, breeds familiarity – and that in turn breeds boredom.

If feet of clay exist, they must never be discovered. The Queen Mother gave a supreme demonstration of the value of inaccessibility on her eightieth birthday in the summer of 1980. From dawn, crowds began to gather outside her home, off The Mall, and by mid-morning the number of well-wishers had swelled to several thousand; parents with their young children, babes in arms and old-age pensioners, they all waited for the grand appearance.

The Queen Mother might have been tempted to make several forays into the crowd to thank them. But, no, the 'appearance' was timed for 11.00 a.m. and on the stroke of that hour she appeared on the balcony, dressed regally in her favourite colour – blue – and standing on a footstool so as to give everyone a good view. As she smiled and waved graciously to the people below, I timed the 'appearance'. It lasted just three minutes. Then, in response to cheers from the crowd, she came down to the street, and accepted hundreds of birthday cards and bouquets of flowers from the hands of small children. That, too, lasted three minutes.

She disappeared inside Clarence House, and the crowd reluctantly dispersed, sighing among themselves in the aftermath of what they had just seen. Had the Queen Mother stayed an hour, the magic would have vanished. As it was, the ordinary folk who had waited for that brief glimpse were grateful for it and ready to return another year.

The grace and charm of the Queen Mother does not come instantly, and Lady Diana was only a beginner. But in those few months together, the professional taught the amateur the ground rules of the most difficult art in the world. Lady Diana remembered her first 'five-finger exercises' that day at Sandown Park, when a voice in the crowd called, 'Congratulations, Di'. Lady Diana accepted the greeting with a smile, but reprimanded gently: 'It's Diana actually.'

Prince Charles may call her Di, and he does; the Queen may, if she wishes, but not you or me. The lady was learning.

It is probably fortunate for Lady Diana that there have been no other Princesses of Wales in living memory with whom she can be compared, favourably or otherwise. No one will be able to point a critical finger and say, 'That isn't how it was done before.' The role will be very much what Lady Diana wants to make it. It is inevitable that throughout her life, she will live in her husband's shadow. But that does not necessarily mean that her personality will be obliterated altogether. Prince Philip, as Consort to the Queen, has proved that on many occasions. Prince Charles is unlikely to find that he has a compliant wife as his companion through life.

More than a century ago, when Prince Albert of Saxe-Coburg became Consort to Queen Victoria, he assumed admirable humility when he described his view of how he should behave. 'The role of Consort,' he wrote, 'has inherent limitations and frustrations. One must impress, but not too much. One must be prominent but not too prominent. A Consort is a fighter who must always be willing to pull his punches.'

It was a keenly observed analysis, and he went on: 'The position requires that the husband shall entirely sink his individual existence in that of his wife: he should aim at no power by himself for himself; should shun all attention, assume no separate responsibility before the public but make his position entirely a part of hers.'

In fact, in time he became the power behind the throne.

The decisions of the monarch were as much his as Queen Victoria's herself.

Lady Diana may not wish to go that far. But neither will she 'sink her own individual existence' in that of her husband. Lady Diana may have a shy, retiring nature but behind it is a steel nerve. No one who saw her cope so superbly with the pressures of her courtship would take her for a push-over. However submissive her role is supposed to be in public, in private she is certain to have a say in many of her husband's decisions. No man is a hero to his wife, and many believe that Prince Charles is fortunate to have found a partner with the perfect touch of down-to-earth experience to bring a new warmth to the aloofness of the monarchy.

Lady Diana also has youth, vitality and a sense of fun which could inject new spirit into the nation as it approaches, with some apprehension, the end of the twentieth century. One hopes she will not allow herself to be changed too much. That giggle would be a sad loss.

There are those who have said that they pity Lady Diana's future, describing it as 'daunting', even 'bleak': the endless round of garden parties, flower shows, civic receptions; and the punishing schedule of royal tours. That is, I think, a pessimistic view and a foolish one. Lady Diana needs only to bring into her royal life the enthusiasm and joy she has shown in the past, for those duties to become a positive delight.

Her love of children is well known, and as well as having her own family she will be able, through the prestige of her position, to encourage and develop more facilities for handicapped children, the under-privileged and the mentally ill. Few people are blessed with such influence, and the exercise of it can only serve to bring Lady Diana a great deal of happiness and satisfaction.

During the long years that Prince Charles will have to wait for the Crown, he will have at his side a loving wife and a caring friend, without whom the burden of his office could become intolerable.

Lady Diana, for her own part, has no fear of the path

ahead. 'With Prince Charles beside me,' she said, 'I cannot go wrong.'

God Bless the Prince and Princess of Wales.

# Postscript

The *Sun*'s exclusiveness on the romance between Prince Charles and Lady Diana Spencer, and later their engagement, mattered little when set against the events themselves.

But they had their rewards. On the day of the engagement I sent a telegram on behalf of myself and Arthur Edwards to Prince Charles and Lady Diana containing the message: 'No couple deserved greater happiness.'

It was just one among the tens of thousands which they received from throughout Britain and the rest of the world. But it was among a comparatively small number which the Prince selected for a personal reply.

He telegrammed: 'Many thanks from us both for your very kind message. Trust you won't be made redundant. Charles.'

He need not have worried. Later, he said to me, 'I suppose now that I'm getting married, you'll start on my brother.'

'Of course, sir,' I replied, 'and if he takes anything like as long as you, we won't be out of work for years!'

# NEL BESTSELLERS

| | | | |
|---|---|---|---|
| T037061 | BLOOD AND MONEY | *Thomas Thompson* | £1.50 |
| T045692 | THE BLACK HOLE | *Alan Dean Foster* | 95p |
| T049817 | MEMORIES OF ANOTHER DAY | *Harold Robbins* | £1.95 |
| T049701 | THE DARK | *James Herbert* | £1.50 |
| T045528 | THE STAND | *Stephen King* | £1.75 |
| T065475 | I BOUGHT A MOUNTAIN | *Thomas Firbank* | £1.50 |
| T050203 | IN THE TEETH OF THE EVIDENCE | *Dorothy L. Sayers* | £1.25 |
| T050777 | STRANGER IN A STRANGE LAND | *Robert Heinlein* | £1.75 |
| T050807 | 79 PARK AVENUE | *Harold Robbins* | £1.75 |
| T042308 | DUNE | *Frank Herbert* | £1.50 |
| T045137 | THE MOON IS A HARSH MISTRESS | *Robert Heinlein* | £1.25 |
| T050149 | THE INHERITORS | *Harold Robbins* | £1.75 |
| T049620 | RICH MAN, POOR MAN | *Irwin Shaw* | £1.60 |
| T046710 | EDGE 36: TOWN ON TRIAL | *George G. Gilman* | £1.00 |
| T037541 | DEVIL'S GUARD | *Robert Elford* | £1.25 |
| T050629 | THE RATS | *James Herbert* | £1.25 |
| T050874 | CARRIE | *Stephen King* | £1.50 |
| T050610 | THE FOG | *James Herbert* | £1.25 |
| T041867 | THE MIXED BLESSING | *Helen Van Slyke* | £1.50 |
| T038629 | THIN AIR | *Simpson & Burger* | 95p |
| T038602 | THE APOCALYPSE | *Jeffrey Konvitz* | 95p |
| T046850 | WEB OF EVERYWHERE | *John Brunner* | 85p |

NEL P.O. BOX 11, FALMOUTH TR10 9EN, CORNWALL

Postage charge:

U.K. Customers. Please allow 40p for the first book, 18p for the second book, 13p for each additional book ordered, to a maximum charge of £1.49, in addition to cover price.

B.F.P.O. & Eire. Please allow 40p for the first book, 18p for the second book, 13p per copy for the next 7 books, thereafter 7p per book, in addition to cover price.

Overseas Customers. Please allow 60p for the first book plus 18p per copy for each additional book, in addition to cover price.

Please send cheque or postal order (no currency).

Name ..............................................................................................................

Address ..........................................................................................................

.........................................................................................................................

Title ...............................................................................................................

While every effort is made to keep prices steady, it is sometimes necessary to increase prices at short notice. New English Library reserve the right to show on covers and charge new retail prices which may differ from those advertised in the text or elsewhere.(5)